Don't
Sleep
Through
the
Revolution

Foreword by

BILLY GRAHAM

An editor's prickly thoughts
on what Christians are here for

WORD BOOKS

WACO, TEXAS—LONDON, ENGLAND

DON'T SLEEP THROUGH THE REVOLUTION

Library of Congress Catalog Card number: 69-20225

First Printing—July 1969

Second Printing—January 1970

Scripture quotations marked RSV are from the Revised Standard
Version of the Bible, copyrighted 1946 and 1952 by the Division of
Christian Education of the National Council of the Churches of Christ
in the U.S.A., and are used by permission.
Quotations from *The New English Bible, New Testament,* copyright ©
The Delegates of the Oxford University Press and the Syndics of the
Cambridge University Press, 1961, are used by permission of Cam-
bridge University Press.
Quotations from *The New Testament in Modern English* by J. B.
Phillips, copyright © 1958 by J. B. Phillips, are used by permission
of The Macmillan Company and Geoffrey Bles, Ltd.

FOREWORD

Dr. Paul Rees has been one of my closest friends and counselors for many years. In the earlier days of my ministry I used to go early to get a seat in the First Evangelical Covenant Church in Minneapolis to hear him expound the Scriptures. His life and ministry have had a tremendous influence upon my own life and the lives of thousands of others.

Dr. Paul Rees illustrates the joy, thrill, and challenge of New Testament Christianity both in and out of the pulpit. Just to sit with him for an hour is always a spiritual tonic. He and I have spent many hours in years past in prayer, Bible study, and spiritual fellowship; and even the memory of one of those hours brings a thrill to my heart.

In 1954 and 1955 I invited Dr. Rees to join me for crusades in Great Britain. We stood side by side and proclaimed the gospel to tens of thousands of people in Britain. It was not long before he had endeared himself to the British evangelical community. From there, his ministry began to extend to every continent until today he is one of the most sought-after preachers in the world.

Few men speak as well as Dr. Rees. But he has achieved the rare gift of writing as well. His personality comes through in every paragraph and leaves people reaching for new heights of Christian living. He jabs the conscience and challenges the mind. Yet in his speaking and writing, the love of Christ comes through clearly, leaving no harshness.

Few men are so adept at metaphor, illustration, and picturesque speech. Utilizing these tools, he holds the interest, he probes and cuts like a skillful surgeon "piercing even unto the joints and marrow."

This book contains the very cream of Dr. Rees's writings,

compiled from his challenging editorials in *World Vision* Magazine. From scores of refreshing and pithy editorials, the publishers have done a superb job of selecting the most significant. In them he has discerned, penetrated, and analyzed the new trends in the Church's world mission with its changing, shifting patterns.

Dr. Rees comes to grips with most of the great problems the Church is facing today. For example, in "Black Man on the Balcony" he confronts the racial problem with honesty, candor, and imagination. Human suffering, eschatology, death, and even Vietnam, come into new focus under his vivid scrutiny.

Paul Rees has written many other books, and they have been enthusiastically received by the Christian community. But in my opinion, this is his best work—partially because it was not meant to be a book. Just the reading of the manuscript has given me new insight as to the adequacy of the gospel when applied to complex modern problems in every cultural situation.

Every minister, every missionary, every observer of the current world church scene will consider this volume a "must" on his book list.

Many of these articles are controversial—they were meant to be! It was Dr. Rees's intention to arouse evangelicals out of their apathy and indifference. In my judgment he has superbly done just that.

It is my prayer that this book will be widely distributed and that it will challenge thousands of evangelicals as it has challenged me.

BILLY GRAHAM

CONTENTS

INTRODUCTION

The Turbulence of a Title

"Don't Sleep Through The Revolution!"

"Rip Van Winkle's 20 years sleep, his rusted gun, and his unhappy return to a world which has forgotten him are subtly symbolic." So says the *Encyclopaedia Britannica* in its assessment of Washington Irving and the whimsical character in the *Sketch Book* who will be remembered as long as American literature lives.

The Revolutionary War was on, and Rip Van Winkle slept it out. "Incredible," you say. Not exactly. Not if you will look around you and see how many citizens there are who are strolling like sleepwalkers through the crashing, bashing, lashing times in which we are living.

And let's not think that all of these benumbed souls are outside our churches. The saints too can be a somnolent breed. Not the real ones, to be sure, but the painted ones. They can warm a pew for a comfortable hour on Sunday and on Monday freeze 20 million American Negroes with a dry-ice cliché about "niggers who better learn to keep their place." Thus the revolution—on just one of its many fronts—gathers momentum, but they go sleepwalking, too unaware either to fear the worst or to pray for the best.

We only play a grim joke on ourselves if we imagine that these are not profoundly revolutionary days. Try looking at your current reading matter. See how many times "revolution" and "revolutionary" turn up as noun and adjective. In less than an hour's browsing I had encountered these:

"The Revolution in Morals"
"The Sexual Revolution"
"The Meaning of Latin American Revolution"
"Christian Witness in a Revolutionary World"
"The Negro Revolution"
"The Revolution of the Economically Depressed"
"The Revolution of Underdeveloped Nations"
"The Gospel of Revolution"
"The Cybernetic Revolution"
"The Technological Revolution"
"In Theology the Order of the Day Is Revolution"

Nor does this tell the whole story. Many an author uses many a synonym for "revolution." He will employ such expressions as "rapid social change," "population explosion," a "crisis of confidence," the "student rebellion," the "knowledge explosion."

All of these phrases, whether actually involving the term "revolution" or not, are relevant, substantial, verifiable.

Take just one of them—the cybernetic revolution. Cybernetics is a branch of modern learning that concerns itself with relationships between man and the machine, more specifically between the human factors and the technological factors in the age of automation on which we have entered. In 1964 a group of 32 economists, labor leaders, and business men drew up a manifesto, entitled it "The Triple Revolution" (cybernation, weaponry, human rights), and sent it to the White House. They wondered if it would be lost in the shuffle. Next day it was on the front pages of the *New York Times* and the *Washington Post*. Yet the full impact of what the manifesto says and implies has only begun to take effect. In a short time the force of its facts and forecasts will be felt on every continent. And the imagination is staggered.

Right in the midst of writing these lines a report has been laid on my desk from a missionary of the Africa Inland Mission who works deep in the late-blooming heartland of Africa—the Central Africa Republic. He writes:

> In the materialistic age where Africans are crying out for a gospel which not only affects their souls but affects also their material well-being, we are finding that we are losing many of the younger generation to a life that is completely separate from the church. Many of the older men in the town of Obo, where we live, requested that we offer some sort of training in a trade.

Result? A Christian trade school where youth will discover that the gospel is not for disembodied "souls" but for *people* in that marvelous body-soul synthesis in which God has made them. True as it is that "man shall not live by bread alone," it is likewise true that he cannot *normally* live without it.

By no means does this illustration cover the whole ground in today's revolutionary world. It scarcely hints at other stages and further implications of the revolution.

What it does say to us is that, in the language of a very much "with it" American folk song, written by a young Minnesotan, Bob Dylan—"Something's blowin' in the wind." And it might be added that in some places it is "blowin'" so hard that you are reminded of the character in *Green Pastures* who shouted, "Everything that's nailed down is comin' loose!" The informed and convinced Christian knows that it isn't but there is enough truth in the outburst to make that Christian offer a witness of toughness and a prayer of tenderness. The witness? "Blow on, wild wind! My faith is made for gales. I defy you to destroy it!" And the prayer? "Christ of tempests, help me to do more than survive. Help me to understand and serve."

Well, our understanding will have to take into account a variety of revolutionary situations that are emerging sharply in this second half of the twentieth century.

1. Consider, for example, the radically altered *cultural-political* context in which mission and missions must be carried forward. Here the key word is *reversal*. (I use "mission" to suggest the calling of the whole Church to world evangelization and "missions" to suggest the plurality of those organized forms that the "mission" historically takes.) In rough approximation the modern era of "foreign missions" starts with the closing years of the eighteenth century. Western man, which at that time meant *European* man, was drinking the heady wine of empire. Imperalism was not a naughty word. Colonialism, far from being a pariah, was a prince. And European powers were wearing more and more of the trappings of their ambitious and possessive princeliness. The Spanish were at it, the Portuguese, the Dutch, the Germans, the French, even the Danes, and, on the most colossal scale, the British.

For good *and* ill the world of the nineteenth century was the white man's world. In varying forms and measures he ruled its peoples, developed its industry, shaped its politics, cultivated its science, fought its wars, taught its medicine and hygiene, controlled its commerce, exploited its natural resources, filled its seas with ships, and slashed its continents with roads.

It was on such an outward flowing tide—from West to East and South—that modern foreign missions floated in the nineteenth century and in the early years of the present century. This tremendous current of European and (later) American expansionism —the *flag,* the *fleet,* and the *francs*—provided the favoring current on which thousands upon thousands of Western missionaries went to Asia, Africa, and Latin America. And precisely here comes the point that I am attempting to bring into sharpest focus: *this tide is no longer running.*

Indeed, that is an understatement. The tide has reversed itself. It is, generally speaking, running against missions. Minority rule by white men over colored majorities—despite present contradictory and antiquated exceptions—is as dead as the proverbial dodo. "Missionary Go Home," splashed on bridges and public buildings, may be taken as the work of nationalist radicals. But the missionary, along with the mission board in London or New York, makes a serious blunder if he misreads the deeper, wider meaning of that ugly slogan. White prestige in a world of color is at an all-time low! If our thinking is not geared to this unhappy phenomenon, we are sleeping through the revolution.

2. Revolutionary too is the new *religious* context within which the work of Christian mission must be done. Its key word is *resurgence*. Until the present century, and well within it, it could be said that for hundreds of years Islam, Hinduism, and Buddhism have been nonaggressive, non-missionary, in character—contrary, of course, to what they once were. Such a judgment can no longer be made. All three of them are astir. All three of them are updating—their own form of what Pope John XXIII call *aggiornamento*. All three are playing down what was weakest in their past, playing up what they feel is most appealing and relevant in their present. All three are forming links with the new nationalism. All three accentuate their identification with a nation's cultural heritage. All three can thereby stress the foreignness, the intrusiveness, the unnaturalness, of Christianity.

Dr. J. T. Seamands, professor of missions at Asbury Theological Seminary, gives an address in which he suggests that, taken in their present mood and method, Hinduism is making a slogan of *tolerance,* Islam of *brotherhood,* and Buddhism of *peace.* Allowing for a certain nebulousness in all generalizations, these are not without evidence to support them. For example, ex-president–philosopher of India, Dr. Radakrishnan, is a brilliant advocate of syncretism; the boast of Islam is that there is no color-bar in its mosques; and the Prime Minister of Burma, seeing the words "Jesus Christ the Hope of the World," flatly tells a friend of mine that this is not so, that it is the Christian West that has embroiled mankind in two world wars in one generation, and that Buddhism is the world's hope for peace.

Whatever the mixture of factors, one thing is clear: here are three non-Christian faiths that have rubbed the sleep of centuries out of their eyes and are on the march. They are prepared to challenge the claims of the Christian Church. Informed persons tell us that there are large areas in Africa, north of the equator, where the primitive peoples are being won to Islam ten times faster than they are being won to faith in Jesus Christ. If we want to be jolted from an Asian source, there is the hostile verdict of K. M. Pannikar, in his *Asian and Western Dominance:*

> It will hardly be denied that, in spite of the immense and sustained effort by the Churches with the support of the lay public of the European countries and America, the attempt to conquer Asia for Christ has definitely failed.

Here is a phase of life in our revolutionary world in the midst of which the Rip Van Winkle role is appallingly out of place.

3. Furthermore, the mood of revolution marks the *economic-sociological* setting of contemporary world evangelism. Its key word is *resentment.* A Southern Baptist missionary in Ghana has told how he learned of the assassination of Dr. Martin Luther King. His informant, only hours after the slaying, was a 20-year-old Ghanian student, who could not report the news without tears in his eyes. The next day the *Daily Graphic,* which is read by virtually every literate Ghanian, let loose such blasts as these:

> They have murdered Martin Luther King at last. We knew they were going to do it, for the murder of leaders of Afro-American movements for equality of all races in that country is a symptom of the disease from which America is suffering. . . .
>
> They started murdering black people . . . a long time ago. Only the Father above knows how many bodies of our kinsman have been thrown into the Atlantic Ocean from the first day the wooden ships set sail from our shores with their cargoes of black men. . . .
>
> Is it our fault that we were made black by the Creator in whom most American whites profess to believe?
>
> The time is long past when leaving for Africa with the Bible in the armpit was a mark of supreme sacrifice. There is still a supreme sacrifice to be made by missionaries—but this does not lie in crossing the oceans to far-away places with strange sound-

ing names. The sacrifice lies right at the door-step of the missionary's own home, wherever it may be in this world.

We who are missionaries can offer the rebuttal that we should never leave our home base at all *if* we waited until our society was clean. Unfortunately, in the existing circumstances this may prove to be less a refutation than a reflection of our own defensive hang-up. After all, the Ghana editor was making no attempt to take clean aim with a rifle. In outrage he was flinging a grenade, with little concern as to where the verbal shrapnel would tear the flesh.

The resentment of the colored races against white assumptions of superiority has now become a global phenomenon. Whether violent or restrained, it sharpens and shapes much that is taking place in the decision-making circles of Africa and Asia. Are those of us who are white Christians insensitive to this explosive fact of our time? Or, to mention something worse than insensitiveness, are we *misinterpreting* it by, let us say, putting all the blame for it on the Communists? If so, we are simply sleeping through the revolution.

Resentments that gather round the race issue are compounded by resentments that relate to what in Latin America is frequently described as Yankee imperialism. It is a kind of successor to political colonialism. It is, for example, the Department of State in Washington, so fearful of the Communist threat in Latin America that it appears to side with the rich and exploitative elite that in nation after nation holds the real power and exercises it to their own advantage. A highly knowledgeable Christian leader, Ruben Lores, is acutely aware of this situation. He spoke for a growing number of our Christians in the nations to the south of us when he dealt with the topic of "Social Justice" before the thousands of young people who attended the Seventh Inter-Varsity Missionary Convention at Urbana, Illinois, in December 1967.

The economic picture of Latin America that he put together for them had these highlights: (1) only 3 percent of the land tillable, (2) only half of that 3 percent actually under cultivation, (3) absentee land-ownership to a phenomenal degree, in Chile 2 percent of the population owning 52 percent of the land and in Brazil two thousand people owning land enough to make collectively a territory larger than the combined area of Italy, Holland, Belgium, and Denmark, (4) this landed aristocracy constituting an "establishment," a power pattern, which, reinforced by the Roman Catholic Church, is tied in with government.

Result? In the words of Ruben Lores, "Today all over Latin America there is turmoil for a change not only of the *conditions* but of the *patterns*. We must have either accelerated political evolution or a chaotic revolution. We must have fair international trade agreements on the part of the United States and the European nations, or else frustration under a stagnant economy."

Yet I have heard some of my fellow Americans, laboring as missionaries in Latin America, dismiss the social and political unrest around them as simply the work of the Communists. If our social insights go no deeper than that, we are reenacting Rip Van Winkle—sleeping through a revolution. Such missionaries, I should hasten to add, are a smaller and smaller minority.

4. Finally, it should be realized by all of us, it seems to me, that our task is now set in the midst of a revolutionary *Christian* context. Its key word—perhaps not the happiest—is *readjustment*. We are in the beginning, for example, of a *theological* readjustment in which the *wholeness* and *unity* of the Church must be far more convincingly manifested than heretofore. In *Protestant Crosscurrents in Mission* Dr. Arthur Glasser, of Overseas Missionary Fellowship, writes:

> The unity of the church is directly and significantly related to her worldwide mission. This is revealed in our Lord's prayer recorded in John 17:20-23. His concern was that his people may "all be one" and know him to be the one sent by God. This confronts us with the imperative to pray and work for an authentic ecumenism that is both scriptural and apostolic, a unity "in truth and holiness." By authentic ecumenism we do not mean something pragmatic, based on either doctrinal indifferentism or the mere yearning for bigness for its own sake. Nor do we mean a

kind of oneness that exists only in the spiritual realm (the invisible church.) We believe there is scriptural validity for seeking to remove the fragmented character of the people of God so that their oneness in Christ might be clearly and visibly displayed. (Abingdon, 1968, pp. 198, 199.)

Note the carefully balanced formulation of Dr. Glasser's conviction and concern. Yet if it were to be taken seriously by our appallingly fragmented conservative evangelicals, it would be dynamite. During most of the twentieth century our fecund multiplication of missionary organizations and small denominations has been practiced under the dubious banner of "No Birth Control!" What is so distressing about it, from the theologian's point of view, is that behind most of it is a seriously defective conception of the nature, the wholeness, and the unity of the "body of Christ," the Church. When we are pressed on the point of our disunity, we flee to the blessed realm of the invisible. Then when the pressure is off, we return to the dividedness and the competitiveness and (not infrequently) the quarrelsomeness with which we operate in the really crucial realm of the visible.

Meanwhile, all over Asia and Africa our Christian nationals are asking, with rising insistence, why these Western divisions and subdivisions of "churches" and "missions" should be imposed upon them. They should ask it. More, they should refuse the imposition. To be blind to this point, to defend the old patterns, is to be asleep in the midst of the revolution.

On the other hand, there are *tactical* readjustments that stand in urgent need of being made. To some extent they are being made—under the pressure of events. But the pace will be quickened as the insights are sharpened. Consider an instance. Ben Wati, of New Delhi, for years the general secretary of the Evangelical Fellowship of India, recently elected president of World Evangelical Fellowship, writes about missions in India as follows:

Only four years ago ... speaking to a group of missionary language students, I tried to impress upon them that they were in India for the next forty years, and so they might as well settle down and get the language. But the world-shaking events of our time make me wonder if the short-term missionary is not now the answer.

Wati goes on:

> The fact that a number of missionaries in India are seconded or on loan from one mission to another, or from one project to another, seems to indicate that the identity of a given missionary body is changing perceptibly. The idea of a united mission appears more challenging, whereby a certain project is visibly attempted. In India the days of church planting through missions are practically over.

Obviously, then, tactical and administrative readjustments must become the order of the day. It is an inescapable part of the agenda that the Lord of history is writing for His witnessing people. If this be true, then let our missionary administrators, whether denominationally related or "faith mission" related, feel the bite of this additional sentence from Ben Wati: "It is an unsavory fact that most missions are painfully slow to move with the times."

Could it be that they have a tendency to sleep through the revolution?

Enough has been said, surely, to underline the turbulence of our time and, accordingly, the turbulence of the title this book carries on its cover. Where the world mission of the Church is concerned it is impossible to escape the fact that we are part of the first generation of the atomic age. The setting of our on-going task has incredible novelties about it, as we have seen. The cultural-political climate, the social-economic climate, the religious climate, and, more restrictedly, the Christian climate—all are different from what they were when this century was young.

It is of course both necessary and salutary to remind ourselves that "in a very real sense our message never changes. There is but one covenant of grace proclaimed and ratified by God. There is but one redemptive act of God whereby sinful men may be justified before a holy God. There is but one invitation to be addressed to man: 'Repentance toward God and faith toward our Lord Jesus Christ.' "

The quotation is from Arthur Glasser. Such a reminder has a certain essentiality about it. It must never, never be forgotten. Yet it is not enough! True as it is and, in some quarters, timely as it is, it is not enough, as no one would be quicker to agree than Dr. Glasser himself.

This changeless message, in terms of its communication, must take account of the radically altered context in which the communication is being made. This is biblical, Pauline, Christian. The "same Spirit," but "differences of administration!" To the Jew "I became as a Jew," to the Gentile, as a Gentile! "All things to all men" in order to "win" them! If you are centrally sound in message and motive, you can afford to be unorthodox in your methodology. You can afford to break with old patterns. You can afford to innovate.

Let me, therefore, suggest a few things that I firmly believe would help us to cope more courageously and competently, under God, with the shatteringly revolutionary time through which we are passing. In some sentences clarity will have to be sacrificed to brevity.

1. *We are urgently in need of better semantics.* Today's theological and ecclesiastical word market is cursed with a particular kind of glut: it is overstocked with ambiguities. And conservative evangelicals are its victims too. "Church," "unity," "ecumenical," "apostasy," "mission," "missions," "evangelical," "fundamentalist," "liberal"—these are words whose definition must be sharpened greatly if we are to have decent, constructive conversations among Christians generally, and not least among conservatives whose essential conservatism lies in their loyalty to the classical Christian creeds—Apostles, Nicene, Athanasian.

The commerce in words is currently in confusion. Surely there must be somewhere a door marked: "Enter the Clarifiers."

2. *We are crucially in need of some first steps in the direction of manifest Christian unity.* We should be bold enough to ignore

the extremism of the one-big-church enthusiasts and yet set about to form actual mergers of groups (denominations and mission agencies) wherever there are already present those marked affinities of doctrine, history, and practice that would make such a union a "natural." Lutherans have been doing it, to their credit. The Wesleyan Methodist and Pilgrim Holiness denominations have recently done it, to their credit. The churches of the Mennonite family should feel the challenge to get together. The same must be said of "congregational" and "free church" groups. As for missionary agencies that lie outside the denominational orbit, they are critically "on the spot" overseas, whether they are aware of it or not. They are perpetuating a pattern of overlapping, duplicated effort, poorly developed personnel, and financial waste. They display a tendency to escalate fancied theological differences to the level of barriers that have no justification in fact. With the rarest of exceptions, further proliferation and division are not a mistake: they are a scandal. Cooperation, correlation and, beyond either of these, actual union would immensely improve the image of our Lord's "body" in the lands where the whole Christian community is still but a small minority.

3. *There needs to be a bold foray into the territory of missionary research.* Far too much of our work is done in needless ignorance of the historical, anthropological, sociological, and missiological facts of life. What the computer people call the "systems approach" to any enterprise should not be laughed out of court by those who wish to protect piety by downgrading rationality. Have no fears: men will never be "born again" by means of computers! Nothing in technology will have put the Holy Spirit out of business. The fact remains, nevertheless, that computerized research can give us vastly better access to useful information in the light of which the saving evangel can effectively reach a larger number of those who today are without the knowledge of the blessed Lord and only Savior.

4. *Finally, we acutely need to put an end to the unbiblical artificiality of certain distinctions of which we have made much*

in the past. The distinctions are there, but we have overplayed them. Saving souls is spiritual; ministering to bodies is less so, if indeed it is spiritual at all. So we have thought and so we have acted. Concern for individuals is evangelical; concern over the social situations of which individuals are inescapably a part is probably "liberal." So we have felt and so we have functioned. Or tried to!

Meanwhile, the biblical concept of man has suffered serious distortion and damage. Man as man is neither body or soul; he is *both* in a living synthesis. He is neither private individual nor social organism; he is *both* in a living blend. If we are authentically Christian, nothing that is authentically human is beyond the pale of our concern. Say, if you wish, that "holy worldliness" without the transforming Cross of Christ is simply "worldly." But don't stop there. Be willing to say also that correct speech about the Cross of Christ which does not issue in "holy worldliness" is neither "holy" nor "worldly." It is escapism.

Dr. Carl F. H. Henry, in *Christianity Today,* has recently done an article that deserves high praise for the insights on which it focuses and the courage it manifests. It is called "Demythologizing the Evangelicals." It concludes with a quotation from Dr. E. Stanley Jones' book *Abundant Living,* written in 1942:

> "The early Christians did not say in dismay: 'Look what the world has come to,' but in delight, 'Look what has come to the world.' They saw not merely the ruin, but the resources for the reconstruction of that ruin. They saw not merely that sin did abound, but that grace did much more abound. . . . That same sense of confidence must possess you if you are to pass from an anemic, noncreative, nay-saying type of person to one who is master of himself and his circumstances and his destiny. But this confidence and faith must not be based on a self-hypnosis, a mental and spiritual fool's paradise. . . . The whole secret of abundant living can be summed up in this sentence: 'Not your responsibility, but your response to God's ability.'"

To which Dr. Henry adds this rapier-thrust:

If you are not satisfied with the way E. Stanley Jones, or

Billy Graham, or this present lesser luminary, holds out hope to this present generation, then for heaven's sake, for God's sake and the Gospel's sake, don't exhaust your energies in indexing their faults—which are many—but light a brighter light and live a life of greater power.

So be it! To the greatest glory of the God who

Lives
Reigns
Redeems
And infinitely cares!

PART I

MISSION
IN
PERSPECTIVE

The Future That Matters

When times are tough and risks are high, the workers in any enterprise are bound to ask, What of the future? Is our cause a loser, or will its final chapter be written in the glowing script of achievement?

The late Robert Ruark, trenchant fashioner of the scornful phrase, turned his literary fury on the "stupidity and arrogance" of the contemporary Africans. He wrote of them with haughty disdain. Not surprisingly, he saw no future for the missionaries and would, on occasion, suggest that if they had any sense they would pack up and go home. Let candor add that more than one missionary had his moments of wondering if Ruark was not a better advisor than the secretary of missions.

The decisive battle

What is needed, in times when crisis assaults faith and difficulty spawns doubt, is a fresh examination of the New Testament, that utterly amazing book of realism and hope. Specifically, we need to nourish our flagging courage on the unique view of past and future which the New Testament discloses. Let's call to our aid Professor Oscar Cullman, who puts the case like this:

> The decisive battle in a war may already have occurred in a relatively early state of the war, yet the war still continues. Although the decisive effect of that battle is perhaps not recognized by all, it nevertheless already means victory. . . . Precisely this is the situation of which the New Testament is conscious. . . . The revelation consists precisely in the fact of the proclamation that that event on the cross, together with the resurrection which followed, was the already concluded decisive battle.

Dr. Cullman goes on:

> This then means that the hope for the future can now be supported by faith in the past, faith in the already concluded decisive battle. That which has already happened offers the solid guarantee for that which will take place. The hope of the final victory is so much the more vivid because of the unshakably firm conviction that the battle that decides the victory has already taken place.

From the biblical point of view, the church of our Lord, the whole community of believing confessors, is literally an *interim* agency. It is the Church "between the times": the time of our Lord's First Advent and the time of His Second Advent. The witness it bears during this interim period is concerned not merely or mainly with ideas and ideals. It is concerned with *events:* a birth, a death, a resurrection, an ascension.

The writer of Hebrews insists that when Christ died, rose again, and ascended, God so *acted* that no identical action will ever again take place for the reason that it will never again be required: "But this man, after he had offered one sacrifice for sins for ever, sat down on the right hand of God" (10:12). Looking back, says the writer, the Cross-and-Resurrection event has a finality that makes it unrepeatable.

But the sentence does not end at that point where we have paused. It concludes with the triumphant words, "from henceforth expecting till his enemies be made his footstool," or, as Weymouth has it, "waiting from that time onward until his enemies be put as a footstool under his feet" (10:13).

Sin and death have been overcome. The kingdom of evil has been dealt its deathblow. This is not hope; it is history. When Christ comes again, as come again He will, it will not be to *decide* a victory yet to be won; it will be to *disclose* a victory already achieved. This is the message the Church is to proclaim to the world. And this is the confidence with which the proclamation is to be made.

Objection overruled

Recently, in Dublin, the sight of Trinity College reminded me of Charles Ranson's moving story about a friend who, as a student there and nearing graduation, told his principal tutor that he intended to go to the mission field. The tutor exploded: "Good God, man! You can't do that! There's no future in it."

Forty years later, after a lifetime of service for Christ among the outcaste people of Tamil country in India, bearing their burdens, struggling with them in their poverty and disease, leading them to the Savior, nourishing them in their often feeble, faltering faith, he one night recalled the angry professor's caustic protest: "There's no future in it."

"But," he confided, "I have found here the only future that matters!" Just so! The Christian's future is already here, bound up in that mighty past when the Lord of glory took a cross and with it made of himself humanity's Man of destiny.

Time's Horses Gallop

In a *Wall Street Journal* cartoon there is an evening scene in which a wife says to her husband: "The plumber was very pleasant to talk to. We chatted for hours." Having but lately felt the pain of paying a plumber's bill, I had no trouble getting on the cartoonist's wavelength.

But there's more than a chuckle here. There is a solid challenge. Time is expensive. It's the chitchat that can be so terribly cheap, so tiresomely trivial.

Time is *mystery*. Nobody can get on without it, yet everybody has difficulty explaining it—including the philosophers. We require all sorts of adjectives in order to refine and illuminate it: work time, leisure time, day time, night time, good time, bad time and endlessly on. A lecturer in philosophy under whom I once studied defined time as "the form of thought under which we relate events to each other and to ourselves." Perhaps you disagree. Try a definition of your own. It isn't as easy as buying a pencil in a dime store. There's mystery here.

Time is *opportunity*. The Greeks had a word for time (*chronos*) which might be translated *duration*. But it said nothing about quality or character. From this word we derived "chronometer"— a timepiece. But the Greeks had another word for time (*kairos*) which meant *meaningful* time or, even stronger, *critical* time. This is Paul's word when he speaks of "redeeming the time" (Eph. 5:16).

We have plenty of chronometers in the world. Our need is for "kairometers"—devices for telling us how critical or opportune are the situations in which we find ourselves. For example, a friend of mine, who teaches theology in an Asian country, has written, "*Now* is the *kairos* of American disengagement in many ways and in many places around the world." Agree with him or not, his use of *kairos* is consistent with that of St. Paul.

God offers us the seeing eye and the open mind, but we are slow to take tests for our color blindness or to order a prejudice to move over and make room for a new idea. So the opportunity for *meaningful* achievement is missed.

Time is *equality*. In the durational sense, time plays no favorites. It levels us. It bestows its favors impartially: 60 seconds to the minute, 60 minutes to the hour, 8760 hours to the year. You have as *much* time as I do. I have as *little* time as you do. It's the management of time—not its measure—that makes the difference between us. Arnold Bennett wrote about "Living on Twenty-Four Hours a Day." That's what everybody has to live on. It is time's compulsory democracy.

Time is *relativity*. This is not to be a "trip" into the far-out physics of Einstein. Our meaning at the moment is much simpler, much closer to the fingertips of ordinary mortals. Is an hour for Johnny over his books the same as an hour on the ball field? In a jail cell time *crawls;* under a romantic moon it *flies*. Your watch will gauge it the same way in each situation but not your emotions.

Whole communities of people—nations, if you will—are sometimes caught up in the relativity of time. Speaking of the swift industrialization of urban Africa, Canon Max Warren writes:

> Here is a revolutionary change of outlook, different from what has occurred elsewhere only in the telescoping of the change into so short a period of time. What proceeded gradually in the Western world over several thousands of years is, in Africa, occurring in the lifetime of the individuals. The bearing of all this on the task confronting the Church in Africa is obvious.

Communicating the gospel and planting the Church must be seen in the new frame of reference created by these fast-moving times.

Time is *urgency*. Jesus felt it: "I must work the works of him that sent me, while it is day: the night cometh, when no man can work" (John 9:4). Pioneer missionary Robert Moffatt felt it: "We shall have all eternity in which to celebrate our victories, but we have only one short hour before the sunset in which to *win* them."

1. We urgently need more laymen with a sense of mission. They could start with Frank Laubach's *Wake Up or Blow Up!* or Lew Davis' *The Layman Views World Missions.*

2. We urgently need fewer missionary societies. Let's blow the whistle on new organizations and do something sensible about blending and merging a good many that are already on the field. It would cost in pride but it would save us dollars—and in Christian image.

3. We urgently need faster transfer of responsibility and leadership from foreign missionaries to indigenous leaders. Some areas might profit by the withdrawal—at least for a while—of *all* the missionaries. Let them be redeployed in unoccupied areas where they can profit by lessons learned "the hard way" in the places from which they have come.

4. We urgently need a rebirth, among Christians of the West, of a sense of responsibility for the Church worldwide. But this new child must be baptized a *servant,* not a *master.*

And the time is *now;* for, in Richard Le Gallienne's vivid phrase, "Time's horses gallop down the lessening hill."

Suffering in Two Settings

The scene: northeast India, not far from the East Pakistan border where Hindu and Muslim refugees are streaming back and forth and bitter emotions pack every moment with violent possibilities.

An observer on the other side of the border wrote:

> In the waterlogged fields of the Ganges Delta children were catching minnows with nets as big as themselves. They were not playing truant from school, because they have no schools to go to. And they were not catching minnows for fun, but for the family dinner.
>
> For most of the 43 million people in East Pakistan, the average diet consists of 18 ounces of rice a day, salt and chili peppers,

and, if they are lucky, about two ounces of minnows once or twice a week.

On this food-pittance, grownups and children, when they are not prostrate with malaria, tuberculosis, kala-azar, elephantiasis, cholera, labor from dawn to dusk in the flooded rice fields or in the jute fields. It is back-breaking work. . . . There is always the danger of famine. The slender diet depends on rice, and although the Delta is a rice-growing area, it cannot grow enough for its dense population.

Suffering! In an area and on a scale that could be duplicated in many another part of Asia!

Imagine my jolted state of mind when I picked up an Asian newspaper and began reading an editorial entitled "Cost of Suffering."

Swiftly assuming that the editor would be grappling with some aspect of privation and pain in this teeming and often tortured part of the world, I was ill prepared for what was in store.

"The Bel Aire district of Los Angeles," the writer opined, "is like no other district in all the world. You casually cast a stone (if you can find one on the immaculate roadside, that is) and a dozen millionaires are hit. A pedestrian is a curiosity, to watch whom there will be found a dozen high-powered celebrities in multicylindered automobiles."

Warming to what proves to be his unexpected subject, our editor recalls that in the era—now well-dated—when private swimming pools were status symbols, "many Bel Airedales [at the least he could have put that innuendo in quotation marks] boasted three pools—one for guests who liked cold water, another for those who preferred tepid water and the third for those who did not swim."

But surely, one thinks, this has nothing to do with suffering. Quite the reverse, one feels.

Very well. The editor is ready to get to grips with his theme. He will *prove* that his editorial is not a misnomer.

The news wires, it seems, have reported that two Bel Aire neighbors have got into a quarrel. There being no other civilized recourse, they have dragged each other into court in a mutual suit in which each is determined to get damages from the other for "emotional suffering."

Now this species of pain, our editor points out, is obviously something that must be distinguished from the common variety of suffering to which all flesh is heir. This brand of pain—the ache of the affluent—is well-nigh priceless.

It must be, since one complainant demanded $25,000 for suffering caused by the other's six-foot fence which, he claims, obscured his view.

The other neighbor assesses the value of her suffering at $39,000, the cause being that the defendant's swimming pool was built a shade too close to the property line between them. Result? The defendant's gardener had unceremoniously cut down some of the branches of the complainant's trees.

The editor, from his Asian chair, observes wryly that money and ingenuity should have no difficulty correcting either of these complaints—for example, by jacking up the house to a height that would command a better view and moving the swimming pool, tile, chrome, and all, to a new location.

"The main point," says our editor in conclusion, "is that these people should not be allowed to suffer, poor things."

One feels like moralizing. Is it necessary?

One feels like preaching. Is it appropriate?

One feels like challenging. Is it required?

Let him who will, begin to draw out the implications—for the Church, the American society, and the millions of "haves" wherever found—of these two pictures of suffering.

I'm Suspicious

I'm suspicious. It is even possible that my suspiciousness is increasing. While I am a long way from being neurotically or chronically distrustful—a piece of self-judgment which I offer at whatever risk there may be in it—I am frankly suspicious.

I'm suspicious of the *snide* as a device for use in serious discussion. The snide phrase or sentence is one that is slyly, often sarcastically, disparaging. When I was a college sophomore, a pungent and powerful editor by the name of Colonel Harvey ran a colorful rightist journal called *Harvey's Weekly*. He could toss off sentences whose rhetoric coruscated like Roman candles on the night of the Fourth. He could sharpen a belligerent phrase that rammed home with the thrust of a bayonet. One of his favorite rhetorical tricks for blasting the old League of Nations was to call it the "Plague of Notions." To my sophomoric mind that was great stuff. Harvey had me in his camp: I was against the League of Nations. And now, half a century later, I know how snide was that phrase. It was far more a writer's trick than it was a logician's craftsmanship.

Yet this kind of thing takes place with considerable frequency in our assemblies of the evangelical faithful. We employ the snide against our opponents who are absent in order to elicit a smile from the credulous who are present. And I am suspicious. I strongly suspect that it is a below-the-belt tactic.

I'm suspicious of the *simplistic* as an instrument of serious discussion or debate. Simplism is a state of mind in which one is content to achieve solutions by artificially extracting the complexities from the problem to be solved. Some time ago one of my dear friends deplored the reluctance of some evangelical leaders to align themselves with a particular group of Christians. By their failure to affiliate, it was contended, they were chargeable with "ecclesiological neutrality." It was further claimed that this position of theirs "exposes them to the influence and gravitational pull of large ecumenically oriented bodies around them where their witness for the gospel might then be neutralized. We must make every effort to get these evangelicals aligned and active in our association where their faith, voice, and numbers may count."

Unfortunately it is not quite so simple as that. Some of the most arresting addresses given at the Berlin Conference on Evangelism came from the lips of men who are in "ecumenically oriented" churches—men who, it may be added, are as forthright in their witness elsewhere as they were within the favorable confines of the Berlin *Kongresshalle*. It is probable that some of them have more influence at more levels of the Church's life than they would if they were to renounce their lifelong connections with their own denominations and go full-throttle for what is offered in an association of evangelicals. It is an oversimplification of the ecumenical issue of one evangelical to say categorically to another, "Break with your church," or, conversely, "Never leave your church."

I'm suspicious of the *suppressive*. This is a technique of discussion wherein you magnify evidence that appears to support your point while you conceal evidence that would either destroy your point or change the shape of it. Thus a radio preacher complains loudly that a council of churches has used its influence on Washington to prevent his fundamentalist group from getting accreditation as a relief agency. But at no time in the bitter broadcast was it acknowledged that other evangelical groups have received the accreditation in question. These facts were suppressed, leaving the uninformed listener with a highly distorted view of the case.

Or—to put the shoe on the other foot—here is a *Christian Century* contributor who declares, "Fundamentalism's acceptance of Scripture as a reality is the basis on which it repudiates higher criticism." "Higher criticism"! A loaded phrase, of course. It lands you spang in the middle of semantics. Plenty of "fundies" and plenty of "non-fundies" would be hard put to give you a respectable definition of the phrase. But that is beside the point. What is suppressed in the quoted sentence is the simple fact that there *are* fundamentalist writers who know what "higher criticism" is and who pay respectful heed to it. Wick Broomall's *Biblical Criticism* is a random illustration that comes swiftly to mind.

I'm suspicious of the *shallow*. Here is a lady who, after years of zealously working for missions in her home church, makes a

trip to East Africa. She insists that the visit had a shockingly dis-
illusioning effect on her:

> I have been wasting my time all these years, knitting clothes
> for people who have no need of them, giving money for a Church
> which has plenty of rich members, with better houses and better
> cars than we have, who only put a penny in the collection on
> Sunday. Not another gift for missions, not another working
> party!

That intemperate outburst is in fact incredibly shallow. Who
ever said that Christian missions consisted of taking the surpluses
of the lucky and laying them charitably on the doorstep of the
unlucky? Even in prosperous Nairobi the dear lady could have
found ghastly poverty. To help relieve it in Christ's name would
be one form of Christian witness. But it is not the main reason
for the Christian presence in Africa—or anywhere else. More
than clothes, Africa needs Christ. To be with or without Christ—
this brings us to the crux of mission. To miss this is to paddle
in shallow waters.

The snide, the simplistic, the suppressive, the shallow—devices
that all bear close scrutiny. Jesus made much of *truth*. As His disciples, it is our business to insist on a better handling of that
priceless commodity.

The Terror or the Torrent?

The reign of terror held in the hot hands of China's youthful
Red Guard appears to have become too senselessly violent even
for leader Mao Tse-tung, its mastermind. It is of course much too
terroristic for the more sophisticated Chou En-lai, who, as one
newsman put it, has stood "at the head of the government's thrust
toward moderation."

Tempting though it may be to remark at length on the absurdities, atrocities, and obscenities of the Red Guard, it is another line of thought entirely that I find most attractive. In order to get on its wavelength I want to quote from a distinguished Roman Catholic writer of our day, Dr. Y. M. J. Congar:

> The missionary torrent is a torrent of love, for the Father's sending the Son into the world is a deed of love. . . . The object of the Church's mission, is the object of Christ's, with this difference, that salvation has no longer to be purchased but to be communicated.

Two comments spring to mind, the first of which has but secondary relevance here. If we read into the phrase "the Church's mission" a Protestant understanding of "Church," then only praise can pass our lips for so fine a statement of the nature and object of the Christian mission to the world.

It is, however, another phrase of Dr. Congar's that has us really "turned on" at the moment: "a torrent of love"! That, says he, is what the missionary torrent is. The phrase is as felicitous as it is feelingful. It has a galloping and gripping effect. And, needless to argue, it is highly supportable from Scripture.

"God so loved that he gave . . ."! And the giving—with Calvary at its heart—was not a trickle but a torrent.

"The love of Christ constraineth us . . ."! And if you know the man Paul who said that, you know that the experience of which he speaks was never for him a tepid thing but something torrid and torrential.

Twentieth-century man is choosing between two intensities: the irresponsible intensity that is destructive and the responsible intensity that is redemptive. The pitiable souls for whom the latter half of this century offers no decisive place are the placid and the passionless, the lukewarm and the lackluster.

Lest we be misunderstood, let's make it clear that love's torrent is *controlled*. Its chief control is the mind, that is to say, the disposition, the character, of Christ our Lord. Whatever charismatic claims may be made for it, it is not a kind of exotic intoxication that magnifies the unintelligible and the weird. This is being written after more than two weeks in India, where a friend of mine saw a man, borne aloft on other men's shoulders, with his head jerking and his eyes rolling. When my friend inquired as to what was wrong with him, the religious devotees who drooled in his presence replied that he was "God-intoxicated." Let's never confuse *that* with the purposeful—though never pallid—intensity of Christ and His friends. "The spirits of the prophets are subject to the prophets," says Paul in a context in which the chief concern is disorderliness in public worship.

Love's torrent, moreover, is *cleansing*. There are proud passions whose effect is to puff us. The effect of Christ's love is to purge us. It must, if it is to rule us; for, as Paul has it in his exquisite hymn of love, "Love is never boastful, nor conceited, nor rude" (I Cor. 13:5, New English Bible.) A pious mother, handicapped by arthritis, after surrendering her egocentric desire to dominate her family (for their good, of course!) was cured of her arthritis. Love did it—love released at a level deep enough to deal with self. Many a frustrated servant of the Church, at home or overseas, needs a similar cleansing.

Love's torrent, we must see, is *cruciform*. The channel within which it flows takes the shape of the Cross. In Douglas Webster's latest book, *Yes to Mission,* we are given a discerning and luminous quotation from the Anglican theologian F. W. Dillistone. Dillistone recalls that in Mauriac's novel *The Lamb* there is a character who says, "Yes, I know that love does exist in the world. But it is crucified in the world and we with it." Regarding this insight Dillistone observes:

> So we are brought back to Mauriac's central message—that whensoever and wheresoever the sufferings of Christ are reproduced in one of His servants, there salvation is being worked out; the salvation both of the sufferer and those for whom he is suffering. Christ's act is supreme, definitive, unapproachable. Yet it cannot be effective in the world today unless it is brought near through its re-enactment in the lives of saintly figures such as Xavier.

At some point in the world of mission this "re-enactment" is taking place every hour. Not long ago I learned of an instance of it in a land long sealed against the gospel. An honorably but delicately prepared scheme for indirect Christian witness was frustrated when an ex-missionary turned diplomat contrived to block it. Was love's torrent withheld? Not at all. But for an agonizing little while the shape of its course was that of a cross.

Dr. Congar is right: "The missionary torrent is a torrent of love." And, in the end, its grim alternative—as Mao's minions have shown—is a torrent of hate and havoc.

Back to Mission—Or Forward?

"When you get back to preaching the gospel, I'll be back in church." The speaker was a businessman who was answering a question put to him by his pastor.

The pastor—from whom I got the story directly—had announced one Sunday that he would preach a series of sermons on what was then more popularly known as "foreign missions." The first sermon in the series had been preached, following which the pastor noted that this man was conspicuous by his absence as subsequent sermons were delivered. It was the minister's inquiry that drew the curious reply: "When you get back to preaching the gospel, I'll be back in church."

It might be retorted that what this layman needed was to get back to foreign missions. But did he? Is it not far more likely that he was typical of multitudes in our churches whose elementary need is to go *forward* to missions? They cannot go back to where they have never been. To borrow a contemporary phrase, they need to "get with it."

Partly, but only partly, our problem is that of defining missions and of educating the millions in our churches to a biblical understanding of what it means to spell out Christian evangelism in global terms.

The missionary enterprise is partnership with God, no less. It is partnership with God in a relationship in which He uses us—we who have found Christ to be a gracious Savior—to publish the good news to men everywhere. It is all this with a view to seeing those who will put their trust in Christ gathered into church fellowships, whose responsibility it will be to tell others who, on believing, will then be gathered into churches that will reproduce their kind. It is the Church in saving action toward and for the world, for which world Christ died.

If this understanding of the matter is sound, then an *insight* is ours, and a principle of action to go along with it, that need not be amended with changes that take place on the cultural, political, or economic scene.

For a long time we have thought of the missionary responsibility as that of the "haves" going to the "have nots," the privileged going to the unprivileged, the free going to the unfree, the rulers going to the ruled. It is worth a moment's reflection to recall that in the beginning of the Christian church and its outreach this was not true. Then it was a case of the ruled going to the rulers, the slaves going to the free, the uncultured going to the nobility, the representatives of the underprivileged classes going to the representatives of the power structures, Antioch going to Rome.

But the objective in both situations should be the same: telling and demonstrating the "good news" of Christ and forming believers into responsible fellowships out from whose warm centers will go streams of living witnesses.

But insight is not enough. There must be *impulse*. There must be a sense of mission. This persuasion must be so strong that everything the Church does is seen as having a bearing on its mission to the world.

The risen Lord, we are told, said to His disciples, "As the Father has sent me, even so I send you" (John 20:21). Forever after it could be said of them: They *went* because they were *sent!* They "missioned" because they had been commissioned.

Mission, it should be understood, is not just exploding into any kind of action. All sorts of action can be detonated that is erratic, irresponsible, destructive.

In the concept of mission there are three ideas that belong together in a living blend: activity, authority, and accountability. The *activity* is whatever it is that forms the core of the assignment. Missions, broadly, are of all sorts: economic, cultural, educational, military, religious. Yet activity alone does not yield mission. There must be an assigning *authority*. The sending requires a sender. And, to form a third ingredient of mission, there remains *accountability*. The President of the United States sends an advisor to Vietnam. His instructions are clear. His responsibility is defined. He goes, confers, examines, evaluates. But the mission is complete only when he reports back to the President.

Our Lord has given his church an assignment. Proclaiming the gospel and gathering believers into reproducing churches are not optional activities. They are laid upon the people of the Great Redemption as something binding.

It is reported that President Franklin Roosevelt, after asking Joseph Davies to accept an appointment as United States ambassador to Russia, sat waiting for Mr. Davies to reply. Impressed by the weighty reasons the President had given for his decision to propose this appointment, Davies said, "Well, Mr. President, it seems to me you are giving me a big job." Promptly Franklin Roosevelt replied, "Joe, I am not giving you a job; I am sending you on a mission!"

Too often, one fears, the members of our churches give the impression that they are just job holders. They serve on committees, sing in choirs, teach in Sunday schools, write minutes for Ladies Aid meetings, and a lot of other things that have their place and value.

Meanwhile, are the men of the world struck by the fact that we are participants in a world enterprise that is at once the most important and the most exciting that ever commanded the energies of human beings? If not, let's get with it!

Let's go *forward* to mission.

The Truth Comes High

Why do Christians have trouble with truth? Not simply with biblical and theological truth, but with truth in general!

The reasons are many. Christians, for example, are still *finite*. Finiteness means limitation. Only God is infinite. The absolutes are with Him and in Him. We may confess them, but we do not fully comprehend them. Even Christians sometimes have difficulty allowing God to be God. They want to assume that role for Him. It never works.

For some Christians difficulties with truth may arise from *lack of commitment*. We may glibly say that we are committed to "the truth, the whole truth, and nothing but the truth," but in fact there are hidden and sometimes hideous reservations. Says a distinguished psychiatrist: "The first law of mental hygiene is this: be honest with yourself." In this realm reservations and rationalizations are a dime a dozen.

Closely connected with lack of commitment is the *reluctance to believe that truth is often costly*. "Buy the truth, and sell it not," we read in Proverbs 23:23. When I quoted this line to a devout lady, she looked mystified. Asked if she realized it came from the Bible, she said no. When she asked me what it meant, I told her that it was a figurative way of emphasizing the priceless value of truth. I could have added that it teaches by implication how *costly* a thing it is to acquire and follow truth. Saul of Tarsus, for instance, found that if he embraced "the truth as it is in Jesus" it would cost him all the favor and standing he had with the Sanhedrin.

Yet another factor that beclouds truth in the minds of Christians is *prejudice*. Prejudice means pre-judgment. It is decision registered before the evidence is all in hand. It is a position taken with only part of the facts admitted. The remainder are either deliberately disallowed or unconsciously ignored. Was the Peter of Acts 10 prepared to take the gospel to the Gentiles and to eat and drink with them in the house of Cornelius? No. He was ready to stand up to the Lord and argue against it. And the reason? Hatred for Gentiles? No. Ill will? No. It was prejudice. At this point his mentality was that of the "establishment." He was for the status quo, no matter how ridiculous the Cross of his Lord had made it.

From these and other considerations several consequences flow. For one thing, we are all challenged, and challenged all the time, to reexamine our commitment to truth. Without fully realizing it, we may be hedging and weaseling. On the other hand, we must be cautious lest we misjudge those whose grasp of truth has not carried them as far as we ourselves have been compelled in conscience to go. Concretely, this would mean refusing to impute to Peter a hostility to the Gentiles which in fact was not there. In the light of the new situation created by the Cross it was prejudice that had Peter in its grip. It was hurtful, to be sure, and it cried out for correction; but it needs to be seen for what it was—prejudice, not perversity.

Truth lays vast claims on all of us. Truth is that which conforms to the reality that God wills in the order of creation of which He has made us a part. It is God in character and God in action. One of the hardest aspects of reality for us to grasp is that in which we see God working out His purpose through men who neither know Him nor confess Him as God. Isaiah does not hesitate to call Cyrus, a heathen ruler, one of God's anointed ones. He was anointed to perform a service in the far-reaching purposes that God had for His people Israel. Thus God declares: "I gird you, though you do not know me" (Isa. 45:5). Thus, too, the arrogant and ruthless Assyrian is called the "rod" of God's anger against Judah.

A case in point is the judgment day that has come to the United States of America because of the long denial of basic civil rights to multitudes of her citizens. If our own people do not know that this is judgment day for us, the rest of the world does. It is easy for those of us who are pious defenders of the old order to cast aspersions on the non-Christian and even irreverent attitude of some of the leaders in the civil rights movement. Easy, indeed, but is it altogether wise? When injustice, hypocrisy, and the subversion of human dignity are at stake, God, in an overruling sense, may be making greater use of the irreverences of a James Baldwin than He is of the outmoded clichés of a United States senator who denounces him.

At the time of the Selma, Alabama, crisis, the President of the United States went before a joint session of the Congress to say, "Yet the harsh fact is that in many places in this country men and women are kept from voting because they are Negroes." That well-documented charge alone demands that the full weight of the Christian community should be thrown behind the insistence that constitutional democracy is not an empty shibboleth but a practicable reality.

As the President said, this is not a Southern problem. This is an American problem. To call it political is to miss its deeper undertones. To call it the work of Communist agitators is to confuse a fractional truth with a far larger reality. To say that the Church should ignore it is to say precisely what pious churchmen said to John Wesley when he fought the institution of slavery in the British Empire.

To hold that Christians, whether they think of themselves as conservative evangelicals or otherwise, can sidestep it, is to hold exactly—and exasperatingly—the opinion held by many devout

Methodists, Baptists, and Presbyterians in the "abolition" fight of a century ago. Defenders of the status quo said then what they say now. Some of them argued flatly: change is wrong. Some of them insisted loftily: change, if it must come, cannot be legislated. Some of them pled pathetically: change must not be hurried.

Yet a hundred years earlier John Woolman, that high-statured, perceptive Quaker, had gone home from a meeting that concerned itself with slavery to write in his *Journal:*

> Many Slaves on this Continent are oppressed, and their Cries have reached the Ears of the Most High. Such are the Purity and Certainty of His Judgments that he cannot be partial in our Favour. In infinite Love and Goodness, he hath opened our Understandings, from one Time to another, concerning our Duty towards the People; and it is not a Time for Delay. Should we not be sensible of what is required of us, and, through a Respect to the private Interests of some Persons, or through a Regard to some Friendships which do not stand on an immutable Foundation neglect to do our Duty in Firmness and Constancy, still waiting for extraordinary Means to bring about their Deliverance, it may be by terrible Things in Righteousness God may answer us in this Matter.

Is it by "terrible Things in Righteousness" that God is now answering us "in this Matter" of American racism?

We are gravely ill-informed if we think that Little Rock and Birmingham and Selma, as well as many an unsavory racist episode in our northern states, have no bearing on the work of the Church in its world outreach and witness.

Let two voices be heard from outside the circle of Christian missions. Less than a decade ago, Mr. Harold R. Isaacs, working as a research associate with the Massachusetts Institute of Technology, produced a book called *Scratches On Our Minds,* in which he warned:

> . . . laugh, cry, or gape, what confronts us is no mere speedy change of scenery, flag, costume, posture, or facial expression, no frantic flashing of new pictures on the propaganda screens. It is the beginning of a change in the underpinning of the total

relationship between Western and Asian and African men. For nearly three hundred years this underpinning was the assumption of Western superiority: a whole vast political-military-social-economic-racial-personal complex was built upon it. Almost every Western image of Asian and other non-Western peoples was based on it. This assumption can now no longer be made or maintained. The whole structure based upon it is being revised. All the power relations that went with it are being changed. This is history in the large, a great continental rearrangement, bringing with it a great and wrenching shift in the juxtapositions of cultures and peoples. Western men are being relieved of the comforts and disabilities of being the lords of creation; Asian and African men can no longer merely submit, nor live on the rancors of subjection, nor revitalize their own societies by the ideas or sanctions of their own more distant past. All must move from old ground to new, from old assumptions to new ones, and as they move must constantly refocus their views. They will all be engaged, for some time to come, in more or less painfully revising the images they have of themselves and of each other. (The John Day Company, 1948, pp. 407-408.)

The other voice is that of Senator J. William Fulbright of Arkansas:

> This question of the moral strength of our people is not just a domestic matter. It has grave implications in our international relations.

The reshaping of our images across the lines of race and color will not take place without resistance. It is conceivable that it will not take place at all—with disaster as a consequence. In this event what will be supremely calamitous will be the failure of the Christian community in the hour when it had its chance to lead the way, to set the pace, to incarnate the truth.

Yes, truth comes high. It is often harsh. It is much easier to settle for a half-truth.

Yet only the truth will ultimately reign.

"Black Man on the Balcony"

The day after the fatal shooting of Dr. Martin Luther King, Jr., a Copenhagen, Denmark, newspaper declared: "The shot in Memphis against the black man on the balcony will signal the beginning of a black summer for the United States of America." This was an understatement. Not for the United States alone nor for that summer alone, but for the whole white world and for a long time thereafter, it signalled the seriously reduced stature of the white man's culture in the eyes of the colored races everywhere.

Five years earlier, not long after the King-led demonstrations in Birmingham, in which the demonstrators were attacked by police dogs and slammed to the pavement by fire hoses, a U. S. missionary to Pakistan was giving an address in a California Presbyterian church. As he finished, he invited questions from the audience. One questioner asked, "What would you say is presently your Number One problem as a missionary in Pakistan?" With no hesitation the speaker replied: "Police dogs and fire hoses in Birmingham, Alabama!"

The world scene is just that sensitive. The race issue is just that explosive. And the death of and violence to the nonviolent Dr. King will add just that much more heat to the thinly banked fires of racial disaster that are ready to erupt in a hundred places round the planet.

There were perhaps five possible ways in which Americans could react to the deed of infamy that took Dr. King's life:

1. They could react with *sheer heedlessness*. They could say, "We are the uninvolved, and we want it that way. We are the unconcerned, and we are content to have it so." Like those who

displayed neither indignation nor sorrow over the ruins of fallen Jerusalem, Americans might well feel the stab of the prophet's question, "Is it nothing to you, all ye that pass by?"

It was either Gilbert Chesterton or someone like him who once said, "Good causes are not lost by being blown up; they are lost by being sat upon." It is the shame of the heedless.

2. They could react with unimplemented *horror*. Momentarily Americans were shocked and shamed. Momentarily they felt grief for Mrs. King and the family. Momentarily they shook their heads and wrung their hands over the violence that plagues our society. But that might be all! Nothing might come of it: no "follow through" in wider prayer, nor conquered prejudice, nor the cultivation of personal friendship with Negroes, nor support for open housing, nor anything else that concretely channels a felt emotion.

3. As a third option, they could react to Dr. King's death with augmented *hatred*. With the killing only 48 hours past, Stokely Carmichael was reported as saying: "Our retaliation won't be in the courtroom but in the streets of America. Black people know that their way is not by intellectual discussion. They know they have to get guns."

Only a trifle less cynical was the bitter quip of a white army corporal: "He asked for it! What good did he ever do for anyone?"

Thus a mounting of black hatred for the whites and white hatred for the blacks could be one form of response to what happened to the "black man on the balcony."

4. A fourth possible reaction could be an authentic *humility*. A phony humility would have the white community saying, "Dear, dear, we have given them so much lately, but it's clear that we must concede them much more." On the contrary, an authentic humility would have the white citizens saying, "Insofar as this struggle is for citizenship rights, we haven't given them anything. We have just been tragically slow to recognize what God and our Constitution have already given them."

5. Humility such as this could lead, by a fairly easy step, to a fifth sort of response: one of creative *honesty*.

Was Dr. King in cahoots with the Communists? If he was, no one has produced a shred of evidence to support it—only surmises, innuendos, and veiled insinuations. The call is for honesty.

Was Dr. King something less than strictly evangelical in his theology? He may have been. I suspect he was at one or two points. So was Thomas Jefferson. So was Abraham Lincoln. But Christ, he believed, held his heart, and the country held his love, and justice held his conscience. The call is for honesty.

Have no strides been made, no strokes of achievement registered, since Dr. King began his "Southern Christian Leadership" crusade in Montgomery in 1956? They have. Measured by nearly a century of foot-dragging and a singularly mischievous form of "cultural lag," the gains have been tremendous. Last year I sat in the restaurant of a new hotel in the heart of Birmingham where, only a few tables away, sat a Negro gentleman and his wife having their lunch. Five years earlier their attempt to enter the place would have created an "incident"—or something worse. These advances must not be forgotten amid the unleashed emotions surrounding the King slaying. The call is for honesty.

There is still, however, a long road to travel. As citizens, of all classes and colors, we need the honesty that drops its masks, flings away its rationalizations, and is prepared to stand up and be counted on the side of civil rights. So it will be that the "black man on the balcony," though lost to our view, will yet see his "dream" come to pass—

... that my four little children will one day live in a nation where they will not be judged by the color of their skin but by the content of their character.

Unsegregated Martyrs

In 1964 the name of Dr. Paul Earle Carlson carried such potent news value that it shouldered bishops and prime ministers from their places in the headlines. How different it had been a few months earlier! Who had ever heard of Wasolo, the site of his tiny mission hospital? And who cared that he was the only doctor for a hundred thousand people in the surrounding area? The Paul Carlson of the early summer of 1964 was unknown to the world, unnoticed by the press, unsung by society—whether African, European, or American.

Then came his arrest by the Simbas, his confinement at Stanleyville, and the trumping up of spy charges against him. The weeks of suspense, during which the world's press held him in a focus that was extraordinary, ended grimly in his death by gunfire late in November.

The subsiding of the phenomenal publicity that attended Dr. Carlson's final weeks of life must have left the thoughtful friends of Christian missions with a disturbing question: Will the message conveyed by this man's life and death strike home in some significantly continuing way to those who most need to get it?

One evening I went with a few friends to visit Dr. Carlson's grave. His body rests in a tiny burial plot only a mile or two from where I had the privilege of addressing the annual conference of the Evangelical Church of the Ubangi. The bronze plaque affixed to the headstone has for its chief inscription John 15:13: 'Greater love hath no man than this, that a man lay down his life for his friends."

From the point of view of contemporary missions the most meaningful feature of this beautiful inscription is that the language used is not English (as it is in the case of other missionaries buried there) but Lingala, the language of the people. Here is telling and timely symbolism. What is symbolized is the principle of *identification,* apart from which the work of the white mission- ary from the West is all but futile in today's Africa. Dr. L. Arden Almquist, who was Dr. Carlson's predecessor at the Wasolo Hospital, speaking at one of the several Carlson memorial ser- vices held in the United States, said:

> Dr. Carlson had, in effect, "stripped himself of all privilege" (Phil. 2:5, Phillips) in order to become a servant of the Con- golese people, even as Christ had stripped himself of the privileges of Heaven to become a man among men upon earth. . . . In so doing, he accepted complete identity with the people he came to serve, a fact they recognized in asking that he be buried among them. "He belongs to us," they said.

While we are speaking of the necessity of being "stripped . . . of all privilege," it should be understood that this includes the "privilege" of having *all* the publicity for martyrdom focused on the white man of God from the West. African Christians have a right to feel that they, too, are paying the price of blood for the ongoing Christian witness. After all, on the very day that Dr. Carlson was arrested at Wasolo, his two wonderful Christian Congolese nurses were killed by the rebels on the spot.

Admittedly, the publicity given to Dr. Carlson's case was mea- sured with an uneven hand. The newspaper psychology behind it is, I suppose, that Westerners are interested in Westerners. Yet the fact that we find it understandable does little to make it less irritating to many Africans. For no one really knows how many thousands of African believers laid down their lives in those difficult years.

Take Pastor Yona, for example, an Anglican minister over on the Rwanda border. A jeep carrying five men arrived one night in front of his house. He and a schoolmaster friend—also a Christian—were ordered to climb aboard. A short distance away, near the bank of a river, they were told to step down. Knowing the fate that was in store for them, Pastor Yona asked permission to make an entry in his diary. "We are going to heaven," he wrote, and then proceeded with care to give the time of night it was, where certain church funds could be found, and so on. This entry completed, he requested that his diary and the few francs he had in his pocket should be delivered to his wife.

One of the rebels was ordered to take him away, but not until he and his friend had sung, "There is a happy land . . . where saints in glory stand." As he was being marched back toward the bridge, he was singing:

> There's a land that is fairer than day,
> And by faith we can see it afar;
> For the Father waits over the way
> To prepare us a dwelling-place there.

At the bridge they shot him and threw his body into the river.

The observant schoolmaster, who at that moment felt sure that he would be next to be executed, remarked about Pastor Yona's murderers: "They were all amazed; they had never seen anyone go singing to his death or walking, as he did, like a man just taking a stroll."

Andrew, the schoolmaster, for reasons the rebels did not give, was released and sent home.

The world knew everything about the death of the white missionary, Dr. Paul Carlson; it knew nothing about the death of an African national, Pastor Yona. Yet, in the reckoning of God they marched side by side in the unsegregated company of the martyrs.

Operation Olympic

The year is 1968.

The event is called the Olympic Games.

The place is Mexico City.

I was there less than a month before the games began. It is doubtful if any country of modern times has taken its responsibilities as the host nation so seriously, enthusiastically, and lavishly as the Republic of Mexico. I saw the 100,000-capacity stadium where the Grand Opening took place on October 11.

As always in this most famous of all athletic contests, the formal opening featured the raising and placing of the traditional Olympic torch. And, as always, the torch had to be carried from the Greek city of Olympia. Runners had to take it to the port of Piraeus, near the storied city of Athens, where the first Olympics of the modern era were held. A ship carried it on to the Italian port of Genoa, where it was the center of attraction in a ceremony conducted at the birthplace of Christopher Columbus.

From Genoa to Barcelona it was shipped. There the runners took over again, carrying it in the heat of summer across the Iberian peninsula to the port of Palos. Here it was placed aboard a Spanish frigate for the long transatlantic voyage to the island of San Salvador, where, according to tradition, Columbus had his first sight of land in the New World. The remaining sea distance was covered by a vessel of the Mexican navy, whose captain handed the precious flame to the waiting runners at Vera Cruz. Their assignment was not easy. Over a high range of mountains they had to climb and then descend to the Valley of Anahuac, itself more than seven thousand feet above sea level. Here at last, where modern Mexico City stands, its high-rise sophistication the pride of its six million citizens, the cheering thousands hailed the placement of that pilgrim flame to signal the beginning of the 1968 Olympics.

There are lessons here for the Christian Church. Paul and other writers of the New Testament would be quick to detect and apply them. Indeed, it is exciting to think that some of the athletic references in the epistles had the Olympic Games for a background. Long before the writing of Corinthians or Hebrews—

at least as early as 776 B.C.—the Greeks were running their Games in the awesome shadow of Mount Olympus.

The Olympic tradition has a *formula*.

Its meetings, held at four-year intervals, are under rules. Its several contests are governed by strict supervision and regulation. Its most distinctive requirement is that every contestant shall be an amateur. This is defined as "a person to whom participation in sport is without material gain direct or indirect."

Let participants in the world mission of our Lord take note. Hirelings and professionals have never been anything but dead weight. The witnessing, redeeming mission has gone forward on the shoulders of men and women, kindled by the Holy Spirit, who have "hazarded their lives for the name of our Lord Jesus Christ" (Acts 15:26).

The Olympic tradition has a *flag*.

The field is white, and it has no border. In the center are five interlaced rings, done in blue, yellow, black, green, and red—the basic colors which appear on the flags of all the nations.

Doesn't that say something to us who belong to the world mission of Jesus Christ and His Church? What is this mission if it is not the taking of the sheer whiteness of God's holy, forgiving love, revealed in the death and resurrection of Christ, and flinging it out into the world with lavish hand and limitless offer? "Whosoever will, let him take the water of life freely" (Rev. 22: 17). There is no "border" around it. "God so loved the *world!*"

The Olympic tradition has a *flame*.

The rays of the sun on Mount Olympus are used to ignite a torch, which is then carried to whatever site has been chosen for the games. There the fire that started on Mount Olympus is used to ignite the official Olympic Flame.

Lower in elevation but higher in excellence than any Olympus was a hill called Calvary. Nailed there to a cross one day was a man they didn't know was God. Strange words often fell from His lips, and one of them was this: "I came to cast fire upon the earth" (Luke 12:49).

And He did it! Into the hearts of His followers He flung the fire of His searching judgment and His sanctifying Spirit and His compelling love.

Nineteen centuries later Dr. Samuel Zwemer, looking back, could say of that part of the New Testament called "The Acts of the Apostles," it is "God's Book of Fire." He adds, descriptively:

> What matchless courage against all opposition! What love for all humanity! What discipline of self in an age of self-indulgence in Rome and Greece! What boldness in proclaiming a message that was to the worldly-wise of their day the acme of foolishness . . .! Yet with it they turned the world upside down— intellectually, socially, and morally, and all in one generation.

The Christ of fire lives on, to be sure. Yet the world today faintly feels it, dimly sees it, for the simple reason that His torch is never well carried in the hands of the torpid and the tepid. It must be grasped by the fingers of the fervent; it must be propelled on the feet of the flaming.

England's poet-preacher, F. W. H. Myers, said of Josephine Butler: "She introduced me to Christianity as by an inner door: not to its encumbering forms, but to its heart of flame."

Its heart of flame!

Lacking *that*, nothing that calls itself Christian is authentic.

The Olympics remind us, then, that the world mission of the Church is best served within a formula of unbribed love, under a flag of borderless universality, and with a flame of purpose kindled at the Cross.

PART II

MISSION PRINCIPLES

Where Went It?

George Buttrick, who has a sense of diction as perceptive as an artist's sense of color, once said that as we have in our large cities a "Bureau of Missing Persons" it might be well if we had also a "Bureau of Missing Words."

Has anyone missed a word of late? It is rarely mentioned. A conspiracy of silence seems to have closed in on it like a muffling, blinding fog.

It is the word "obedience."

An incident underlines the rarity of obedience.

George Barrett, an Episcopal rector in New York, has a book in which he tells about two young ladies who came to him after he had officiated at a wedding. They questioned him about one feature of the marriage ceremony. Both of them were soon to be married. Both wanted to know why the vows which he had required the couple to repeat had not included any promise to obey.

The rector explained to them that when the Prayer Book was revised some years ago the word "obey" was deleted from the vow which the bride makes to the groom. Each of the young ladies expressed dissatisfaction with this change. Each insisted that she *wanted* to make such a promise at the time of her marriage.

What is perhaps even more surprising is to have the rector say that he knew these girls to be "very normal young women, neither of whom was the type of person who would enjoy being ordered around or dominated."

Shades of the Victorian twilight! How incredible to find "normal" people of the second half of the twentieth century putting so much store by anything as dull as obedience!

A look at Holy Scripture recalls the duty of obedience.

God is the one person who has never softened up on this theme. He has talked obedience since the human enterprise began.

He talked it to Abraham: "Thou hast obeyed my voice."

He talked it to Israel: "If ye will obey my voice indeed."

He talked it to King Saul: "To obey is better than sacrifice."

And what says the New Testament?

It tells of Christians who felt the *compulsion* of obedience: "We ought to obey God rather than men."

It tells of Christians who experienced the *blessing* of obedience: "The Holy Ghost whom God hath given to them that obey him."

It tells of Christians who were given a *directive* for obedience: "Obey them that have the rule over you."

It tells of Christians who had a *reputation* for obedience: "He [Titus] remembereth the obedience of you all."

It tells of Christians whose eternal *calling* from God is unto obedience: "Elect according to the foreknowledge of God the Father . . . unto obedience."

Obedience, obviously, is not one of the Bible's marginal themes. It is a major note in its commanding message.

Contemporary culture witnesses to the unpopularity of obedience.

As a broad piece of social criticism it is fair to say that this is not an era of obedience. Parents who yearn to feel "modern" may speak of trusting their children, or guiding them, or leading them, or even challenging them. But they would be embarrassed to speak of governing them.

Many teachers and school administrators have all but abandoned the idea of exacting obedience from students, even in elementary schools. Undisciplined at home, undisciplined at school, they go undisciplined into society.

"But surely," someone says, "the Church is not slack in stressing obedience." The answer, unfortunately, is that the Church too is remiss. A great deal of our shallow religiousness makes of God a convenience, not a commander; makes of prayer a device for manipulating God rather than a devotion in which He masters us; makes of Sunday morning worship a snugly satisfying form instead of a shattering judgment and a healing grace.

The Christian conscience needs to rediscover the excellency of obedience.

Christian obedience is surrender to God's will as revealed in Jesus Christ and set out in Holy Scripture.

Christian obedience is not a spineless acquiescence in some blind, impersonal fate. It is open-eyed commitment to that matchless person, Jesus Christ, who rescues history from fate and subdues it to the purposes of God and the people of God.

Christian obedience is a child of repentance and a creature of faith. It springs to life when the pride of our minds and the arrogance of our wills have been brought to the dust.

And if our obedience falters (as falter it may, though falter it need not), then it is ours to prove the infinite Mercy that pardons and the infinite Holiness that heals.

Where went it—this missing word "obedience"?

The Mission Magnificent

If too many of the world's people are purposeless, too many of the Church's people are missionless. "That the average church member and the typical church have lost their sense of mission is ultimately a judgment upon us who are leaders of the Church," says Robert Raines in his widely read book *New Life in the Church.*

A good antidote for this pathetic missionlessness may be found in the introduction of Paul's letter to the Romans. Paul describes himself as "a servant of Jesus Christ, called to be an apostle, set apart for the gospel of God" (1:1). He then speaks of "Jesus Christ our Lord" as the One "through whom we have received grace and apostleship to bring about obedience to the faith for the sake of his name among all the nations, including yourselves who are called to belong to Jesus Christ" (1:5,6 RSV).

Man with a mission! That was Paul.

One is struck by the *intention* of the mission: "to bring about obedience to the faith."

The eminent concern of God's covenant community, Israel, was to bring about the obedience of *law.* The eminent concern of God's covenant community in Christ, the Church, is to bring about the obedience of *faith.* Faith may be taken to cover both the content of the gospel and the principle on which the gospel is offered and received.

The gospel is filled with, and formed by, the revelation that God has made in His son, Jesus Christ. In Paul's own words, it is "the gospel concerning his Son, who was descended from David according to the flesh and designated Son of God in power according to the Spirit of holiness by his resurrection from the dead." This is the good news: God in Christ has overcome and made atonement for our sins by His death and resurrection.

The principle on which the gospel is both announced and appropriated is that of obedient faith. More than belief, it is trust; more than assent, it is commitment. When the Church fails to proclaim this, with conviction and passion, it ceases to be the Church of the New Testament. As Professor Emil Brunner vigorously puts it (and one does not *always* quote him with approval), "Missions, gospel-preaching, is the spreading out of the fire which Christ has thrown upon the earth. He who does not propagate this fire shows that he is not burning."

Furthermore, one is struck by the *inspiration* of the mission. This inspiration leaps from a phrase in verse 5: "for the sake of his name."

The name, of course, stands for the person. The Church is corporately Christ's embassy in the world, and each believer is individually an ambassador. Recall that moving passage in Paul's second letter to the Corinthians, "So we are ambassadors for Christ, God making his appeal through us. We beseech you on behalf of Christ, be reconciled to God" (5:20).

But we do not get on well with our ambassadorial task if we are simply lashed by duty: we get on well as we are inspired by an immense love and a vast gratitude. "By this we know love, that he laid down his life for us; and we ought to lay down our lives for the brethren" (I John 3:16). This creative and compelling passion flamed in David Livingstone's heart until, near the end, he wrote:

Christ is the greatest Master I have ever known. If there is anyone greater, I do not know him. Jesus Christ is the only

Master supremely worth serving. He is the only ideal that never loses its inspiration. . . . We go forth in His name, in His power, in His Spirit, to serve Him.

Programs may stimulate us; it takes *persons*—in this case the ultimate Person—to capture us.

One is struck, finally, by the *inclusiveness* of the mission: "We have received grace and apostleship to bring about obedience to the faith for the sake of his name *among all the nations.*"

Here the apostle faithfully echoes the mandate given the Church by her sovereign Lord: "Go, therefore, and make disciples of all nations" (Matt. 28:19). All men need the gospel. All men are included in its embrace and entreaty. All men, therefore, should hear it proclaimed and see it embodied.

This universality has sometimes been contradicted by the strange exclusivisms of the gospel's own friends. An Asian Christian, now a distinguished bishop, told us how his father solemnly warned him as a boy not only against trying to enter the white Christians' cathedral but even against being found in the road that led up to the cathedral door. Happily, that strictly segregated day has now passed. The night that I preached in that cathedral two-thirds of the worshipers were Asians.

"The Evangel is for all men," wrote Dr. Samuel Zwemer. "The Great Commission is world-wide in its scope. Nothing human can be alien to the Gospel. He died for all, who died for us. He hateth nothing that He hath made."

Meditating on a Myth

According to sociologist Dennis H. Wrong of New York University, it is time that we took a second look at that phenomenon of man which has to do with the increase of his numbers on this planet. By whatever name we may call it—"population explosion," "population bomb," the "swarming of the earth"—it has given rise to a number of misconceptions, which Professor Wrong calls "myths."

One of these erroneous ideas, we are told, is that the population explosion "has resulted from a rise in the birth rate in the countries of rapid growth." Birth rate has indeed had something to do with it, but, especially in Asia and Africa, this is a secondary factor. In practically all of the underdeveloped countries, Professor Wrong insists, "The crucial factor has not been a 'baby boom,' such as we experienced here after the war, but rather a sharp drop in the death rate."

Ceylon is cited as a case in point. So swift has been the introduction and effective use of modern medical and public health measures that this country's death rate dropped as much in the year 1947 as it did over a period of fifty years in the nations of the West during the time that they were passing through their own "modernization process."

If we can assume that Professor Wrong is right (the pun is deliberate but not derisive), and the assumption is a fairly safe one, several assorted reflections are suggested:

1. If the use of scientific means for preventing the conception of life is, in any and all circumstances, morally wrong, being, as opponents of birth control put it, an "interference with nature," why is it not also unethical to *prolong* life by interfering with nature in the use of scientific medicine, sanitation, hospitalization, and all kinds of public health measures? Death control, we are reminded, is more responsible by population pressures and problems than uncontrolled human fertility.

2. Declining death rates in non-Christian lands, so notable, for example, in the case of infants, may yet be shown to have behind them a Christian explanation. Notwithstanding all that belies its claim to be Christian, the West has inherited from Christ and the early Church a sense of the preciousness of the individual

as a creature of God, and, joined with it, a sense of responsibility for being our "brother's keeper." Today, as it penetrates the non-Christian world, multitudes of people who have no understanding of its origin are being influenced by this Christian heritage.

3. Where this sense of the preciousness of the human person is lacking, death control is immediately infused with terrifying possibilities. Russia and China under Communism, and Germany under Nazism, developed the concept of "superfluous people." Demonic as it is, it is consistent with totalitarianism. Ominously, Professor Wrong says, " A continuation of the pressures of rapid growth is bound to heighten the appeal of totalitarian techniques as a form of drastic demographic surgery, for totalitarianism is essentially a method of disposing of social problems by eliminating whatever and whoever makes them." This is not the least of the reasons why many thinkers now regard Red China as far and away the free world's greatest threat.

4. Our final reflection asks for a preface. That preface is that the more than three billion humans now on this planet need to know that the God of creation is also the God of redemption. From this point of view, *how* they got to survive so long here—whether by unchecked human fertility or by scientifically applied death control—is not so important as the fact that they are here in such fantastic numbers. They are here as sinners. They are here in need of forgiveness, peace with God, reconciliation with one another, fellowship that makes for wholeness, and a destiny brightened by hope. In short, they need *saving*—whether white Baptists in Brooklyn or brown Hindus in Bombay.

Hence the piercing pertinence of these stabbing sentences from Dr. Eugene L. Smith, for many years, until 1964, the executive secretary of the Board of Missions of the Methodist Church:

Every age is an age for evangelism. God has no grandchildren. No generation can live on the spiritual experience of its parents. Mankind is always just one generation away from the eclipse of the Christian faith. This danger is the more acute because the form of godliness so often outlasts its content. Institutions easily survive the death of the spiritual awareness which brought them into being. Baptism by water without baptism by the Spirit is preparation for apostasy, which is more dangerous than paganism. Every generation has to be evangelized anew. The task is timeless. The time is now.

Babies and Bibles

Recently I participated in an international Church Leaders Conference called and chaired by the Archbishop of York in his capacity as president of the world's United Bible Societies. For five days the nearly hundred persons who had been brought together—roughly half from the Bible societies and half without Bible society connections—faced up to what Dr. Raju, the United Bible Societies' research secretary, has called the "crisis in world Scripture circulation."

This crisis is compounded of three facts: (1) the population explosion, (2) the literacy explosion, and (3) the wholly inadequate rate at which the Scriptures are being put into circulation.

By the "literacy explosion" is meant the phenomenal progress now being made both in teaching the world's children to read and in wiping out illiteracy among the 500 million human beings between the ages of fifteen and fifty who cannot read. The success of Dr. Frank Laubach and the World Literacy Committee is being vastly augmented by the UNESCO scheme for teaching 350 million illiterates to read within five years.

The urgent question is: What will they read?

Bible society leaders, vividly aware of this situation, have a concern which they rightly suspect is not fully shared by millions of people in our churches. It is concern lest the effort to make

Holy Scripture available to the world's burgeoning population shall turn out to be an affair of "too little and too late."

Facts with which the Conference was confronted were:

1. That in 1962, fifty-one million Scriptures (meaning a whole Bible or a New Testament or a Bible portion) were placed in circulation, and that in 1963 the number increased by only two million.

2. That if this rate of increase were to continue, it would require sixty years to put even a Scripture portion into the hands of the world's people, provided we could make two assumptions: (a) that the world population would stand still for these sixty years and (b) that presently used copies of Scripture would last that long. Needless to say, we can assume neither of these positions. Actually, on the second count, the Bible societies reckon that the "life expectancy" of copies of Scripture is fifteen years for Bibles, ten years for Testaments, and two years for portions (such as the Gospel by John).

As to the projected increase in the number of people needing to have the Scriptures at hand in a translation they can understand at a price they can afford, in much less than sixty years—by the end of the century, in fact—it is expected that the present three billion humans on our planet will have become six billion.

In each second that ticks three babies are born. At each day's end, relatively fewer people are dying. Each year that closes we have added to the human mass the equivalent of an Italy—fifty million.

And against these staggering totals an increase in Scripture circulation of only two million!

True, this figure does not take account of what is being done by such agencies as the Gideons and the Pocket Testament League. On the other hand, its significance must be weighed in light of the fact that in Asia, Africa, and Latin America 95 percent of all Scripture circulation is linked up with the work of the Bible societies.

Modest enough, therefore, is the proposal of the United Bible

Societies to step ahead and to put into circulation a minimum of 150 million Scriptures a year. But if this goal is to be achieved under God, the churches will need to put their shoulders to the wheel and give herculean support to the total effort.

"Up for Grabs"

To what extent the phrase "up for grabs" is what the British call an Americanism, I am not sure. In any case it *sounds* more like New York than it does like Oxford. When rights or properties are to be parceled out, when issues and ideas are open and options on them are allowable, it is sometimes picturesquely said that they are "up for grabs."

This suggests a situation in the world of missions that has been developing for some time, with no conclusive result as yet discernible. It is a matter of vocabulary. The issue, simply put, is between those who say that such words as "mission" and "missionary" are dated and must be replaced, and those, on the other hand, who insist that these words are essentially dateless and need only, therefore, to be reminted and recirculated.

In the United Presbyterian Church, for example, it has been a sort of "official line" in recent years to refer to those who do overseas service as "fraternal workers" rather than "missionaries." Even within that communion there are those who take opposing views of this change.

Without suggesting that the new vocabulary has no good reasons to support it—for I think that it has one or two—I find myself wondering every now and then if we in the churches and in our missionary enterprises are not too quickly convinced that men of the secular world have lost their ability to absorb and understand these time-honored terms of ours.

This thought was recently sharpened in my mind on reading an article by Canon Max Warren, of London, long active in missionary circles and now Canon of Westminster Abbey. For several years Dr. Warren has been keeping a file of clippings from secular sources in which these doubted and debated words— "mission," "missionary," and "evangelist"—appear. They appear, to be sure, not in a theological or Christian context but a secular one. The point is that they are so used as to imply a notably accurate understanding of their basic meaning.

Citing the evidence

Among the examples given are the following:

In the sphere of politics, a letter was published in *The Times* of London which said in part: "If, as a Tory, Mr. Macmillan cares about the future fate of the nation, from now on he must show himself to be a strictly party man and not an evangelist. His present missionary zeal for certain liberal policies is driving it straight into the welcoming arms of those renowned missionaries, the Labour Party."

In the realm of economics, one newspaper described a group of Australian businessmen on a visit to London as "Missionaries of Finance" who had come to "prospect the City," while a trade magazine, describing commerce between Britain and Egypt, said: "Trade missions may do more for the missionaries involved in them than for the cause they were meant to serve."

In the area of technology, a weekly newspaper, referring to the government's Ministry of Technology, asserted that "no one could deny that there was a job to be done and that a way should be sought of bringing the new gospel of technology to the barbaric industrial hordes."

And, of all things, in the domain of doubtful sports, one paper, taking note of the mushrooming of gambling in fashionable clubs, ran a subhead which read, "Bringing Roulette to the Masses." "There's a tremendous future," it declared, "in bringing roulette to the masses. In Mayfair alone there are over sixty clubs undertaking this missionary work; if some die, others mushroom overnight to take their place."

Holding to the point

Let's not be sidetracked from our main thought by exploding indignantly against this prostitution of the word "missionary" through association with the gaming table. What is important to note is that in all of these quotations there is revealed an understanding of the meaning that Christian history has bestowed on these now doubted, and to some degree discarded, terms. The root idea is that of *sending*. There is a message to be communicated, a task to be performed, a goal to be reached—this is the *mission*. Those who carry the message, who engage in the task, who help reach the goal, are therefore *missionaries*. It is as simple as that.

If the day comes when denominations and mission boards abandon a vocabulary that has been in accepted use for two hundred years, they may justify their action on other grounds. Let them not suppose that it is because these terms are too difficult to understand. The pressure to throw them away is being turned on, oddly enough, at the very time when the secular order is ready to take them up.

It just could be that another reason lies beneath the surface. Perhaps we are less sure than our fathers were that the Church of Christ *has* a mission to the world and that every Christian is by nature a missionary.

That could be—mind you, I say *could* be—the disastrous change that has taken place.

Emotions Enter Theology

"We are no longer sure that it is in the plan of God's salvation that the other religions shall die in order to be replaced by Christianity."

Those are the words of Dr. Kaj Baago, professor of church history at United Theological College, Bangalore, South India. They appeared in an article in the *International Review of Missions*.

Before Dr. Baago has finished his article he moves from hesitation to affirmation: he *is* sure—sure that Christian conversion is not necessary among Hindus and Buddhists, that identification with the Church is an expendable concept, and that the saving uniqueness of Jesus Christ has been exaggerated by the colonially minded Christians of the Western world. Dr. Baago asserts:

> If God has not worked and if He does not still work in different cultures and through the religions of men, then He is not the Lord of the world, but a Jewish-Christian idol.
>
> The Christian religion, to a large extent a product of the West, cannot and shall not become the religion of all nations and races.
>
> The missionary task of today cannot, therefore, be to draw men out of their religions, but rather to leave Christianity (the organized religion) and go inside Hinduism and Buddhism, accepting these religions as one's own, in so far as they do not conflict with Christ, and regarding them as the presupposition, the background and the framework of the Christian gospel in Asia.

In owning such thoughts as these Dr. Baago is not alone. He is only more candid, more impatient and more articulate than many for whom he speaks. We only deceive ourselves if we imagine that this is not a growing trend among Asian Christians. I say "Asian," because this development is appreciably more advanced in that part of the world than in Latin America or Africa. Nor, of course, should it be forgotten that Professor Baago's viewpoint is shared by a considerable number of thinkers in our American seminaries.

"Common search for truth"

This very acknowledgment makes it appropriate to say that the Baago position is not startlingly new. It is substantially the same as that which was taken by some of the most influential leaders who participated in the world conference on missions in Jerusalem in 1928. It is the view most commonly associated with the name of Professor William Hocking of Harvard, who headed the so-called Laymen's Inquiry. This in turn resulted in the publication, in 1932, of *Re-Thinking Missions.* The close similarity between the Baago stance and the Hocking position will be quickly detected in the following sentences:

> The Christian will therefore, regard himself a co-worker with the forces which are making for righteousness in every religious system.
> The relation between religions must take increasingly hereafter the form of a common search for truth.

Much more recently Dr. Hocking has produced a book called *The Coming World Civilization,* in which he makes it clear that his views have not significantly changed since he helped write *Re-Thinking Missions.* Just to see the eternal as love, and in a "clean aloneness" to identify with that "timeless reality"—this, for Dr. Hocking, and presumably for Dr. Baago, is the all-integrating point towards which all high religions are moving. To achieve this end Christianity must be willing to give up its claim to the uniqueness of Jesus.

Much has been said, and much more is bound to be said, by way of theological reply to these proposals. If the Christian church, from the apostolic age onward, has been mistaken about Jesus Christ's lordship over history, over nations, and over men, then the sooner it closes its doors and goes out of business the better. Well-reasoned, insightful replies to those who share the Baago-Hocking mind have been given by Hendrik Kraemer in *The Christian Message in a Non-Christian World,* by Dr. Robert E. Speer in *The Finality of Jesus Christ,* by Bishop Stephen Neill in *Creative Tension* (not nearly as well known as it deserves to be), and by Bishop Lesslie Newbigin in *A Faith for This One World.*

Colonialism and imperialism

The comment that I wish to make on the article by Professor Baago is of a different order entirely. I refer to what may be called the *emotional pre-conditioning* that has gone into the writing of the article. The author is obviously resentful toward Western Christians whom he identifies with the whole detestable era of colonialism and imperialism. A good deal of this resentment and cynicism is understandable, some of it wholly justifiable. For example, he quotes from a speech made to the United States Senate, around the turn of the century, by Senator Albert Beveridge of Indiana. To his fellow Americans the Senator cries:

> God has made us the master organizers of the world to establish system where chaos reigns. He has given us the spirit of progress to overwhelm the forces of reaction throughout the earth . . . [and] to administer government among savage and senile peoples. Were it not for such a force as this [i.e., American power] the world would relapse into barbarism and night. . . . He has marked the American people as His chosen nation to finally lead in the regeneration of the world. . . . The judgment of the Master is upon us: Ye have been faithful over a few things. I will make you ruler over many things.

The mildest thing you can say about such jingoist mouthings is that they were culturally premature! The most serious thing to be said about them is that they were theologically hopeless.

The God of history, kind though He has been to her, has *not* anointed the United States to be a twentieth-century messiah.

The crux of missions

Once more the air must be cleared. Once more the issue must be sharply refined. The crux of missions is not religion versus religion nor Western culture versus Eastern. The heart of the matter is this: "What shall I do then with Jesus, which is called Christ?"

Meanwhile, let Western Christians acknowledge that much of what our culture has produced has served to *obscure* rather than *reveal* the "Lord of glory."

Reformer's Blind Spot

About 450 years ago Martin Luther nailed to the door of the Wittenberg Castle Church his 95 theses concerning indulgences— what one journalist called the "first shot in the war of words that was to create the Reformation."

That Luther has become, in the perspective of the centuries, one of the half dozen authentic history-makers of the world is now pretty generally admitted. There has been plenty of time for the assessors to take his measure. Both the eulogists and the muckrackers have had their innings. Sycophants and slanderers alike have had at him. He survives them all. If praise from the "opposition" is sweeter than the fulsome words of fellow travelers, then let the recently stilled lips of the brilliant Jesuit, John Courtney Murray, speak it for Luther: "a religious genius—compassionate, rhetorical, and full of insights."

Yet there was one insight that was missing in Luther; or, if not missing, at least but dimly present and lamely articulated. I refer to the theology of mission and the responsibility for undertaking missionary work. In the 1961 symposium volume entitled *The Theology of the Christian Mission,* Professor William R. Hogg contributed the chapter on "The Rise of Protestant Missionary Concern, 1517-1914." In it he says: "One searches in vain in the *Works of Martin Luther* for any exposition of Matthew 28: 19,20 or Mark 16:15 that would hint at the Church's responsibility to move beyond Christendom."

In another 1961 publication, *Pentecost and Missions,* Dr. Harry Boer, missionary-theologian of Nigeria, drew attention to the same vacuum in the German reformer's thinking and teaching. He quotes Luther:

> What Christians in general and the civil authorities neglect to do with respect to seeking the lost lambs, this the elders of the Church shall undertake to make good in every possible way. *And though they do not have an apostolic call and command to go to strange nations,* yet they shall not in their several churches . . . permit anyone who is not associated with the congregation of Christ to be lost in error.

Luther's view, let it be said in fairness, was shared by some of the other distinguished Reformers, including Calvin, Melanchthon, and Zwingli. They took the position that New Testament references to going with the gospel "into all the world" applied to the apostolic age. When that age ended, the expansion of the Church into "heathen" areas would take place under the heat and pressure of persecution. They therefore found no place for missions abroad as a form of voluntary obedience to the Church's crucified and risen Lord.

Bishop Stephen Neill has an excellent study of missions entitled *The Unfinished Task,* which had its fifth edition in 1961. In it he draws attention to the fact that the Reformers' failure to develop a theology of mission is reflected in the *static* definition of the "Church" which is associated with their names. The bishop quotes from the Seventh Article of the Augsburg Confession: "The Church is a congregation of saints, in which the gospel is purely taught and the Sacraments rightly administered." And he remarks, "Now all this is perfectly correct as far as it goes, but does it go far enough? . . . All the emphasis is on that which is fixed, stable, and unchanging; and it is these elements which most naturally find their expression in a fixed and unchanging organization."

Rightly does the bishop ask, "But is that all that the gospel has to tell us about the nature of the Church?" The answer is No.

As some of the Reformers and most of the Anabaptists and Pietists realized, the Church is not to be a *settlement* but a *pilgrimage,* not an *estate* but an *embassy,* not a *mansion* but a *mission.* The Church's Lord had boldly declared that His Word and Cross and Spirit were to be a "fire" which He had come to "cast upon the earth." It is the business of fire to spread; and, as a rule, in the spreading it is no respecter of barriers.

Luther, in company with a number of the Reformers, was curiously nationalistic in his conception of the Church, whereas, of course, the Church in mission, from Pentecost forward, was to rise above nationalism and to "make disciples of *all* nations."

We salute Luther and his Reformation peers. They deserve it. Their work was incomparably important. But then, remembering our own frailties, we may take warning from their blind spot. "Thine eyes," said the prophet, "shall see the king in his beauty." *This* Luther did. "And," added the prophet, "they shall behold the land that is very far off." *This* Luther did not.

Four and a half centuries later, as the above citations show, this imbalance is being corrected. It would, however, be a thousand pities if we today, seeing the far-off "land" more clearly, see the "King" less clearly than did Luther.

PART III

MISSION
IN
PRACTICE

Words and the Word

Max Muller, I should think, was easily the nineteenth century's foremost authority on the science of language. When in 1873 he was invited by Dean Stanley to lecture on this subject in Westminster Abbey, it was the first time that a layman had ever been accorded the honor of addressing a congregation within those notably sacred walls. German-born, he became a naturalized citizen of England. Oxford-based, he immersed himself in Sanskrit, became an authority on comparative philology (the science of linguistics) and a writer and lecturer on Oriental philosophies and religions. By anyone who takes Jesus Christ as only Lord and Savior, Muller's personal religious faith left much to be desired.

All the more remarkable, therefore, is the following assertion from his *Lectures on the Science of Language,* published in London in 1877:

It was Christianity which first broke the barriers between Jew and Gentile, between Greek and barbarian, between the white and the black. When people had been taught to look upon all men as brethren, then, and only then, did the variety of human speech present itself as a problem that called for a solution in the eyes of thoughtful observers; and I, therefore, date the real beginning of the science of language from the first day of Pentecost. . . . The pioneers of our science were those very apostles who were commanded to "go into all the world, and preach the Gospel to every creature," and their true successors, the missionaries of the whole Christian Church.

For a millenium and a half—a St. Jerome of the fourth century to a Max Muller of the nineteenth—it was the Christian church in missionary obedience and outreach that made valuable contributions to linguistics. True, these contributions were made indirectly, since the primary motive was not language analysis but rather the translation of Holy Scripture and the communication of its message. All this belonged to the pre-scientific period of linguistics.

For the past century linguistics has been repaying its debt to missions. The scientific study of language—its forms, sounds, structures, and cultural colorations—has made possible (1) the production of first-time Bible translations of high accuracy and (2) the spotting and replacing of older translations that were marred by inaccuracies and inadequacies.

For a fascinating and sometimes amusing discussion of this relationship between the revelation of God in Scripture and the technics of language one should read such a book as *Message and Mission* by Dr. Eugene Nida. Take the word "heart," for example. We English readers tend to forget that in many cultures the symbol for "the emotional focus of personality" is not the heart. Among the Chujs of Guatemala it is the abdomen, among the Marshallese it is the throat, and among the Totonacs of Mexico, the spleen. In certain dialects of Northern Congo, John 14:1 reads, "Let not your liver be troubled." Amusing and slightly revolting, you say. Yes, within our present Anglo-Saxon cultural framework. But to these Congolese, meaningful and relevant. And this is what is important in the business of communication.

Said one of the members of the committee responsible for the New English Bible: "The most fascinating thing about translating is that it is so impossible." Anyone with even a thimblefull of knowledge of the problems of the translator will be aware of what he meant. Yet, paradoxically, the supernatural wonder of the Bible is the universal *translatability* of its message.

Roaming with the Researchers

Outward bound for Africa and India, the itinerary calls for a day and a half of "consultation" talks in Brussels. This hub and pride of one of Europe's smallest countries has gone smartly international. It is both the seat of the Common Market and the headquarters for NATO—from the former of which Great Britain is excluded and from the latter of which she is progressively with-drawing. Both matters are very much alive at the moment. What these developments may mean for the future, both of Britain and the continent, who is prepared to say?

On the food front

In the cultural, linguistic, political, and gastronomic mix that is today's world, Brussels is playing its blending part—painfully at times but inevitably. A Congo missionary, temporarily in residence here, was asked by the grocery saleslady what he did with the peanut butter that she was wrapping for him. She winced when he said it was a sandwich spread of which his children were fond. For the same purpose Belgian children want chocolate paste. All very educational—on both sides!

Speaking of wincing, even an American missionary is shaken by the price of food in Brussels. Hamburger comes at $1.50 a pound and beef for roasting is $2.20.

Currently about ninety missionaries, destined for French-speaking Central Africa, are studying in Brussels, most of them working on their French.

Where history meets modernity

What is symbolized when you see a laundromat cheek-by-jowl with an antique shop has its counterpart in the world of the churches and the missions. At the edge of Brussels, for example, stands the famous university town of Louvain. Down a narrow, winding street, within a building that bears no outward sign of being a global nerve center of a kind, I found the offices of the International Federation of Institutes for Social and Socio-Religious Research. In the verbal shorthand so popular today, it is FERES. It has links with research centers in twenty-five nations of Europe, Africa, and Latin America. The number of such affiliated centers is steadily growing. The aim of FERES is to "undertake scientific research in order to analyze and discover the social and religious phenomena at work in contemporary society." Begun as a Roman Catholic project, its scope has been widened to include similar centers under Protestant auspices. By a recently concluded agreement the *World Christian Year Book,* previously published in London, will become the responsibility of FERES.

Looking around at the small offices—their nineteenth-century ceiling heights are greater than their length or their breadth—and taking due notice of the amazingly small staff, one wonders how a project so ambitious and important could be housed here. The explanation, or at least a major part of it, is ultramodern: the computer facilities of Louvain University.

Down Africa way

Next day, in the late December gloaming, BOAC whisked me away for a night flight to East Africa. At 10:30 in the morning, at Nairobi, I was welcomed by a company of some thirty-five specialists who had been brought together by the Rev. Dr. David Barrett, director of the Unit of Research that is based in Kenya. Dr. Barrett, an Anglican clergyman of winsome evangelical persuasion, is probably the foremost authority of the so-called "independent churches"—some would say para-churches or quasi-churches—of Africa. The group displayed, I thought, a lively interest when, on request, I gave a sketchy account of the Missions Advanced Research and Communications (MARC) Center in California. It is a computerized project operated as a division of World Vision International, in cooperation with Fuller Theological Seminary.

I suppose there is danger of making a fetish out of the computer and of thinking that gadgetry is next to godliness. As one whose primary passion belongs to the world of preaching, Bible teaching, evangelism, and pastoral care, I am without technical competence in this new order of scientific research applied to the world Christian enterprise. Yet in my bones I feel its value. Most churches and missions have far too little information on which to base important judgments that affect policy and practice. An abundant supply of facts will still leave us an area of freedom within which the guidance of the Spirit of God will be needed. It takes more than data to dismiss the Holy Spirit.

Array or disarray?

For example, in the short time that I was present in the Nairobi consultation it was discovered that two groups, each without knowledge of the other, were proposing to issue a glossary of terms that are the peculiar property of the Christian world in our time, regarding which, however, much haziness and ambiguity exist. (Try "ecumenical" or "younger churches.") In instance after instance Christian groups have engaged in duplication of effort that represents a needless drain on brains and purses. At Nairobi one was reminded that this sort of overlapping cannot be excused much longer.

Technology: The Titanic Tool

Technology is many things: a Cal Tech laboratory in Pasadena, a General Motors assembly line in Flint, a mock-up of the supersonic Concorde in France, a "cracking" plant in Kuwait, a new hybrid grain in Venezuela, the intrauterine device for birth control in India.

Technology is applied science. And this, beyond anything the human species has ever known, is the age of science.

In no area of man's experience is this phenomenon of technology more socially revolutionary than in the broad field of communications: press, film, radio, television. As Daniel Lerner observes, in his *The Passing of Traditional Society,* "No modern society functions efficiently without a developed system of mass media."

Think of this from the point of view of the *factual*. The plain and immensely important fact is that in publishing, in filming, in broadcasting, and in televising, new records are being set all the time because, on the one hand, the apparatus of production is being improved and, on the other hand, the number of literate receptors is being vastly increased.

The "leap forward" in communications is swift, scintillating, and sometimes shocking. When the communications satellite Early Bird made it possible for the United States to blanket Europe with a strong, clear TV signal, President Johnson, never slow to size up a dramatic situation, asked for prime time to beam a speech directly to Europe. He had later to be reminded that in his haste he had violated diplomatic protocol by addressing foreign peoples without first notifying their governments!

Asia has more than a thousand daily newspapers, with a combined circulation in excess of fifty million. Japan has more than five million television sets. Africa, slowest to feel the impact of technology in communications, is moving ahead with increasing tempo.

Or, think of communications technology from the point of view of what is *potential*. We live in a day when breakthroughs are not terminal. They are but way stations.

The *Saturday Review,* in an early 1966 issue, pays serious tribute to the knowledge and prophetic sensitiveness of General David Sarnoff, chairman of the board of the Radio Corporation of America, who says that he now foresees what the *Review* calls "a one-world concept of mass communication." Sarnoff holds that we are presently able to "transmit across vast distances all types of information—print and picture, the spoken word, telegraphic messages, televised images, and even the esoteric language of computers."

"We are then," say the editors of the *Saturday Review,* "on the threshold of radical change in the ways we communicate everywhere on the planet." They feel that General Sarnoff's suggestion amounts to a call for the "unification of all present communications media—television, radio, newspapers, magazines, and books—into a single integrated electronic medium that would serve a global audience with instantaneous sight and sound."

The mind boggles, the tongue stammers, at possibilities so unprecedented as these.

Or, to carry the matter forward into an area that must always be of concern to the Christian, think of communications technology from the point of view of the *theological.*

One possible biblical implication of the picture and prophecy offered by General Sarnoff is that here we see the stage being set for a future consummate gesture of human pride in the reign of Antichrist. "An earlier generation," Bishop Lesslie Newbigin has discerningly noted, "was inclined to dismiss the New Testament figure of Antichrist with a disdainful smile. To our generation he is an uncomfortably familiar figure, delineated—for instance—in Big Brother of George Orwell's novel, *1984.*"

There is a second implication: Only as technology in communications is informed, gentled, and heightened by the spirit and purpose of Jesus Christ will it be kept from contributing to the future depersonalizing and secularizing of twentieth-century man. At this point Christians must not shirk their responsibility.

A third implication would appear to be urgent: In every lawful way let Christians, in effective concert, take hold of the mass media and work through them to declare God's good news in Jesus in order hopefully to build up in faith and fervor *all* of the people of God, and thus make known among *"all* the nations" the new life Christ gives in a "kingdom" which is "righteousness, and peace, and joy in the Holy Spirit."

It is encouraging to see the IFMA (Interdenominational Foreign Missions Association) and the EFMA (Evangelical Foreign Missions Association) drawing closer together in consultation and collaboration on a variety of interests and projects. But this is not enough. This can leave us in petty contentment. Wider consultations, boldly and imaginatively entered upon, with not the slightest compromise of gospel essentials, are called for by the gigantic issues, threats, and hopes of our time.

Technology is a tool. Let's not surrender it to the wrong hands.

To Spark or to Smother—Which?

"When looms weave by themselves, man's slavery will end." Aristotle speaking—more than twenty centuries ago!

Looms now weave by themselves—this was the gift of the industrial age; but man is *not* free—this is the stubborn theological problem. This indeed is at the root of the Church's continuing mission with the gospel.

Fallen man has an exasperating genius whose chief contradiction is to be seen in his ability to change his environment without basically changing himself. He is now engaged, as a matter of fact, in what promises to be the most astonishing overhauling of his earthly situation since time began. Recently *Saturday Review* published a special issue called "The New Computerized Age." Introducing their theme, the editors wrote: "Few technological developments are formidable enough to mark turning points in history. Two such phenomena have occurred in our time: the atomic bomb and the computer."

"The implications of the bomb," they went on to say, "are beginning to be understood—its capacity for instant and total destruction has been demonstrated. The implications of the computer as yet are only faintly comprehended."

That there are computer-age "implications" that should be faced by our churches and missionary societies is our firm judgment. This judgment rests on such facts as the following:

1. *The computer is here, and here to stay.* Ten years ago, the experts tell us, there were less than a thousand computers in the United States. Today there are forty-three thousand. In the next decade it is expected that this number will be trebled.

2. *The computer potential is fantastic.* "In just ten years," says David Sarnoff, RCA's distinguished authority in this field, "the typical electronic data processor has become ten times smaller, 100 times faster, and 1000 times less expensive to operate. These trends will continue, and our national computing power, which is doubling every year, will soon be sufficient to make the computer a genuinely universal tool."

3. *The computer society is on the way.* According to the *New York Times,* in an article by Dr. Jerome B. Wiesner of the Massachusetts Institute of Technology, "The computer, with its promise of a millionfold increase in man's capacity to handle information, will undoubtedly have the most far-reaching social consequences of any contemporary technical development." It will not be necessary for small offices and private homes to have a computer. Informational systems will be available on much the same basis on which we subscribe for telephone service.

4. *The computer limitations, though few, are crucial.* The computer can develop "bugs." Its intricate circuitry can get fouled up. It can err, though it seldom does. But these are not its critical limitations. Professor Norbett Wiener of MIT, winner of the National Medal of Science for achievement in mathematics, puts his finger on the sensitive area when he declares: "The computer is just as valuable as the man using it. It can allow him to cover more ground in the same time. But he's got to have the ideas."

5. *The computer implications are theologically important.* The image of God in man, though perverted by self-centeredness and distorted by related forms of evil, carries with it a certain gift of creativity.

Connected with this gift are the biblical command to "subdue" the earth and the biblical disclosure concerning man: "Thou madest him to have dominion over the works of thy hands" (Ps. 8:6). True, the New Testament gives us the Christian modification of this outlook upon man when it observes, "But now we see not yet all things put under him. But we see Jesus . . ." (Heb. 2:8,9).

It is, however, neither scriptural nor sensible for us to be dismayed at the succession of "breakthroughs" into nature that the sovereign God is permitting contemporary man to make. Our Christian concern should be that every possible means shall be taken to insure a use of today's technology that is socially constructive and spiritually effective.

6. *Finally, the computer availability for missions calls for understanding and boldness.* Neither computer nor diagrammatic scheme can save a single soul, evangelize a single province, or build a single church. Planning tools such as PERT (Program Evaluation and Review Technique) are not a substitute for prayer. Data processing is not a technique for dismissing the Holy Spirit.

PERT is not so much a method of mission as it is a systematized way of discovering what methods the Holy Spirit has used and is using, and what methods, used or new, are open to Christ's people now as they seek God's further guidance for the completion of the unfinished task.

PERT is capable of giving to missionary leaders and personnel a thoroughness of orientation that the churches have never known. It will not turn us into robots. It will, it is hoped, turn us into roused and resolute missioners, possessing a tool that will add to, not subtract from, our confidence in the living God.

If the technicalities of planning can be used to spark us rather than smother us, a notable victory will have been won.

The Wonder World of Words

Speaking of the Protestant Reformation, H. G. Wells once remarked: "It is not too much to say that paper made that revival of Europe possible."

Paper! Martin Luther's 95 theses spang against the door of the Wittenberg cathedral!

Words! Words reduced to print, serving as holy incendiaries, setting Europe aflame!

Of such is the kingdom of words!

The wonder world of words is a world of *universal humanity.* Living beings communicate. But only *human* beings have the capacity to turn sound effects into a coherent system of symbols, called words.

The wonder world of words is a world of *fundamental psychology.* God has so constructed the human psyche that, for one thing, it is *curious.* It asks questions, it seeks answers. It has a built-in urge to communicate and to be communicated with. It has a leaning toward learning. This fact was never so obvious, never so important on a world scale as now.

According to UNESCO, there are eighty million new readers in the world every year. Long before UNESCO tooled up, Dr. Frank Laubach was putting vigor and vastness into his literacy program. The good doctor's eyes twinkle as he says, "One foolish man asked me how I made the illiterates want to learn. I replied, 'That isn't our problem. Our problem is how to chase them home at night when *we* are tired out.' "

Man's mind, moreover, is *retentive.* Impressions that come to him become part of the mind's inventory. They are retained and recallable—even though the recollection may not be at will.

At this point a significant fact emerges. It is that, other things being equal, we tend to attach higher authority, and therefore credibility, to what we see in print than to what we hear in speech. Also, with many people the recallability factor is heightened. Thus an African, newly literate, insists to his European friend that Moscow is the only city in the world that has a subway rail system. When the European attempted to be equally insistent that other cities had similar systems, the unconvinced African replied, "Oh, no. Moscow is the only city in the world with trains like this. *I read it in a book!*"

It was in print. It must, therefore, be true. Such is the psychology of the printed word, with its singular power to make and to recall impressions. This psychology, one scarcely needs to add, works both ways: for truth or for falsehood, for God or for the devil.

Furthermore, the wonder world of words is a world of *amazing technology.* The entire realm in which printer and publisher operate has been revolutionized in the last thirty years. This is true of every phase of the business—writing, production, art, distribution, promotion.

Can Christian writers and publishers ignore this fabulous development, this colossal phenomenon, of our times? Not unless they want to default to the Communists, the pornographers, and the secularists. John Crispin of the English journal, *The Christian,* is right when he says, "Unless the Christian press is going to be directed at an ever-decreasing minority of people with the time and inclination to wade through unattractive material, it has a responsibility to be interesting." Pertinently, London's *Daily Telegraph* recently commented that the Communist literature being circulated in India was "beautifully produced and ridiculously cheap in price."

We must remember that in literature, as elsewhere, scientific technology is morally neutral. It is simply a tool. Whether it is to be good or bad, virtuous or vile, depends on whose hands are on it for what purpose.

The point should be made, finally, that this wonder world of words is, for the Christian forces today, a world of *staggering opportunity.* In the quarterly journal of the Christian Literature Crusade I saw a list of twenty-three countries in which there are specific needs for literature personnel: translators, production managers, copy writers, teachers for writing schools, bookshop and bookmobile operators, bookkeepers, mail-order supervisors.

All of these technical skills, let it be added, must be illumined by those biblical and theological insights that will give the printed message, whatever its form, the healing grace of a gospel and the enduring relevance of a Savior who is Christ the Lord.

In the first chapter of St. John's Gospel three locations, or forms, of the Word of God are disclosed. In verse 14 we have the Word "made flesh." Here is the *incarnate* Word. In verse 23 John the Baptist quotes from Isaiah 40:3. Here is the *inscribed* Word. Finally, in verse 29, John cries, "Behold the Lamb of God which taketh away the sin of the world." Here is the *intoned* Word.

To alter the order slightly, the Word in *Person,* the Word in *pronouncement,* and the Word in *print!*

And these three, in the wonder world of words, are a telling and triumphant trio.

The Bible: Evangelist in Print

"There is just one book that bears translation into all languages, transmission through all ages, and transplantation to all lands, and that is the Bible." So wrote James Hastings, famed for his *Bible Dictionary.*

In the year 42(St. Jerome, that "most learned of the Latin Fathers," became the first man to translate the whole Bible into the Latin tongue. It was from this translation that Wycliffe worked when, a thousand years later, he produced the first complete Bible in English.

Heroic and noble is the heritage of translations and versions of Holy Scripture to which we are heir—we who are concerned about the penetration of the whole world with the Christian message.

"In regard to this great Book," said Abraham Lincoln, "I have but to say, it is the best gift God has given to men. All that the good Savior gave to the world was communicated through this book."

It was fitting, therefore, that Senator Fred Harris of Oklahoma introduced into the *Congressional Record* an extended resolution of appreciation for the immensely valuable work of all those persons and agencies that, past and present, have contributed to the circulation of Bibles in the languages of men everywhere.

Most of these Bibles are in the vernaculars of the people, a fact that reminds us of the Welsh woman, blessed with but slight education, who insisted that Jesus was a Welshman. They told her, "Oh, no, Jesus Christ was a Jew." "But He speaks to me in Welsh," was her reply.

How right she was!

A Case of Catholic Candor

Thinking back over my reading in the field of mission, I find that one of the memorable books is a slender volume entitled *Missionary Crisis and Challenge in Latin America*. Its author is Robert Wood, a concerned Roman Catholic.

Author Wood gets at the contrast between superficial strength and actual weakness by citing such statistics as the following, based on a total Latin American population of 200 million:

90 percent are baptized Catholics,

33 percent take their first communion,

4 percent of the men, 10 percent of the women, "make their Easter duty,"

70 percent are without basic instruction in the Catholic faith,

50 percent of marriages occur outside the church.

Wood comes to the overall conclusion that not more than 15 percent of Roman Catholicism's claimed membership are active Catholics.

He rightly feels that after 400 years of strong authoritarian presence, overwhelming ecclesiastical prestige, and (often) political power, this is a poor showing. How is it to be explained?

The author faults his church in these particulars:

1. *A bad start.* The Spanish conquerors, looking for gold, were not good representatives of the love of God.

2. *A foreign clergy.* Uruguay, for example, has known times when 85 percent of its clergy were foreigners.

3. *Denial of religious liberty.* He pins most of the blame on the early Spanish leadership.

4. *Dissensions and conflicts within the church.* His account of these controversies and rivalries does much to dispel the myth of Catholic unity and solidarity.

5. *Inconsistencies in the behavior of leaders.* Wood says "they fell into all kinds of abuses, and in many of the remote mountain regions the priests often had families."

With more concern for his side than rancor against those on the other side, the author sees the Protestant movement in the following perspectives: (1) increasing numerically, (2) growing "national roots" which it will be difficult to eradicate or change, (3) going out to the people in direct and sympathetic contact instead of waiting for the people to come to them, (4) wisely stressing the witness of the laity, and (5) displaying as their most conspicuous weakness their divided, confusing, and often competitive, sectarianism.

Robert Wood is a convinced Catholic but a *concerned* one. Protestantism could do with more convinced Protestants who are at the same time *concerned.*

PART IV

MISSION
POLICY

"The Right To Be Heard"

The phrase is taken from Dr. John A. Mackay. It appears in his book *The Science of the Church Universal.* In discussing "The Church's Redemptive Function" he makes the point that Christians are those who, having found something *vital* in Christ, are compelled to be *vocal* for Christ. The community of the transformed must be the community of the transmitting. Here is the *kerygma,* "the Christian message of salvation." And it is *message,* of course, that is indissolubly linked with *mission.*

In this context Dr. Mackay employs the phrase "the right to be heard," adding, "This right is won when non-Christians, or merely nominal Christians, are eager to know what Christians have to *say* because they have learned to respect them for what they *are."* Here, it seems to me, we have an insight and a suggestion that need to be explored.

Obviously "the right to be heard" assumes that one has something to say. "Let the redeemed of the Lord *say* so." Although

Paul was speaking very personally, the Church of the centuries has understood him to have been speaking definitively when he declared: "For I delivered to you as of first importance what I also received, that Christ died for our sins in accordance with the scriptures, that he was buried, that he was raised on the third day in accordance with the scriptures" (I Cor. 15:3,4, RSV).

The gospel is neither a discussion nor a debate. It is an announcement. Discussion may follow along—sometimes helpfully, sometimes detrimentally. What should never be missed or muddled it its "announcemental" character.

Moreover, it is not in the first instance an announcement of what has happened to *me* or to *us*. It is an announcement about *God*—this tremendous thing that God has done in Jesus Christ. Before it becomes something subjective and experiential, the gospel is something objective and historical. When the Church's sons and daughters have grasped this, and are grasped by it, the way is paved for mission. Being now able to say, "We are justified by faith, they can go on to say, "We are ambassadors for Christ."

"The right to be heard," moreover, is related to a psychology in which the person of the speaker is accepted in advance of any acceptance that is given to his message. That this psychological pattern has its occasional exceptions does not invalidate it. Such an exception may be presumed to have occurred in the case of the sudden meeting—with its thrillingly happy outcome—between Philip the Evangelist and the Ethiopian official (Acts 8:26-39).

All extraordinary cases to the contrary, it is true, and notably so in the contemporary situation, that the Christian witness requires for its effectiveness something other than its evangelical content. It requires a climate of personal and group relationships in which respect for the person of the witness precedes reception of the message borne by that witness. Indeed, it is fair to say that this respect may sometimes rest, in the ordering of the Holy Spirit, upon grounds that are unrelated to the gospel.

Take a simple case. Here is a Sunday school teacher in England who finds that one boy in his class of early teens is simply not being reached—nothing gets through to him. Nevertheless the boy *is* reached—when the teacher decides to bone up on guinea pigs because guinea pigs, he has learned, are the boy's hobby.

I know of at least two places in India where Christians, some of whom rank well in the social and business community, have volunteered for the most menial and despised tasks in public hospitals and schools for the blind. In one case a government official, a Hindu, said, "Only Christians will do this work." Evangelism? No, not directly. But pre-evangelism—emphatically! The creation of a climate in which "the right to be heard" is being established!

Finally, "the right to be heard" needs to be theologically understood and exercised. Central to the whole Christian concept of salvation is the declaration: "And the Word became flesh and dwelt among us, full of grace and truth" (John 1:14). If the divinity of man is the conceit of the proud, the humanity of God is the hope of the humble. God stooped; we are lifted. God identified himself with us in our need; we are elevated by Him into a fellowship with Him that—let's say it reverently—meets His need. The identification He made was a precondition of the redemption He now offers.

If we believe in an incarnational theology, then let us practice an incarnational psychology: going where people are, getting next to them, identifying with them, gaining their confidence at some level or another of their legitimate interest.

And please, no posing! The poseur hasn't a chance.

Thus, under God, may we gain "the right to be heard."

Revolution!

The country is Ecuador. The scene is the residence of the Roman Catholic Bishop in Ibarra. Bishop Haro—a new episcopal breed that mothers the poor, champions the oppressed, and works for the exploited—is giving a reception for a visiting clergyman from the United States.

Let the visitor describe what happened:

> The guests were not the affluent merchants of the town, not the hacienda owners, nor be-plumed Knights of St. Gregory in battle array. No, the bishop had gathered around him those closest to his heart—delegates from the festering slums and scrubby mountain farms. One mother broke up the meeting. Weary with worry, malaria, and a nursing baby at her open breast, she cried, "This *palacio* is no longer reserved for the rich from big haciendas. Now it has become *our* house, my house, the home of the poor." This weary mother broke up the meeting because Bishop Haro burst into tears and left the room.

To which the visitor adds: "And so did I!"

The point to note is that something revolutionary is taking place in Latin American Catholicism. A further point is that this revolution within the dominant church of Latin America is a belated response to the burgeoning revolution of social and economic life. And the still further point, which must be grasped by implication, is that this revolutionary hour places upon Latin Protestantism the burden of asking: Is our evangelicalism with all of its verbal orthodoxy demonstrating concern for people as people and not alone for abstract "souls"?

In solemn fact this query should be raised on a global scale. It is appalling how little sensitiveness we North American Christians display toward the immensities of the world revolution through which mankind is passing.

Millons of people are hungry: they are on the march for food.

Millions of people are illiterate: they are on the march for education.

Millions of people are in poverty: they are on the march for a larger share in the bounty of the good earth.

Millions of people are diseased: they are on the march for better medical care, better sanitation, better health.

Millions of people in the world of color are smarting under the arrogance and irrationality of the "white supremacy" era: they are on the march for authentic self-identity, for what some perceptive authorities are calling "psychic security."

What then?

If in gaining these ends God is ignored or denied, the secularized victory will boomerang: nations and cultures will go to hell clutching the fading fruits of their phenomenal successes.

Meanwhile, there is an alternative. It is an alternative that is not well represented either by theological liberals or by theological conservatives. The liberals understand providence and history better than they understand the Cross and the Resurrection. The conservatives understand the Cross and the Resurrection better than history and providence.

In all of the flux of revolution, the liberals in Christian missions are about to put themselves out of a job. They concentrate on education and medicine and agriculture. Now their schools and hospitals and experimental farms are being taken over by government. Missionaries who have been long on proclaiming to men that they need an improved environment and short on telling them that they need a new heart in Christ are now being told in effect, "Thank you, but we know how to achieve the better environment *without the new heart.*"

Where does this leave us as conservative evangelicals? Can we now smugly say, "There, we told you so! It is the gospel that men need above all. Eternity is more important than time and the soul more valuable than the body. Let's not get sidetracked in any social improvement schemes"?

Here precisely is where the evangelical community is in grave danger of committing a fateful blunder. The sentiment expressed is true, but it is irrelevant, because it leaves us unwilling to identify with the "revolution of rising expectations." We are reluctant to give it our blessing. We are loath to say that God's hand is in it. We have developed a theological neurosis in which we are nervously unwilling to combine the social insights of Old Testament prophets with the gospel witness of New Testament apostles.

Now is the time for the whole evangelical world to say to billions of people who are caught in the tension and torture, the harshness and hope, of world revolution:

1. You can have your revolution unredeemed, and plunge into the abyss with it; or

2. You can have it, and we shall *help* you have it, under the lordship of Jesus Christ.

A Pertinent Plea

The Spanish Evangelical Alliance some time ago issued a statement of fact and appeal so deserving of respect that we can only hope for it a wide circulation. Its signers speak responsibly out of the context of the Protestant situation in a nation overwhelmingly dominated, politically as well as religiously, by the Roman Catholic church. Their concern arises from what they feel is the more or less irresponsible way in which outside Protestant agencies have sent workers to Spain when neither the agencies nor the workers had the knowledge, the skills, or the contacts that would make their work effective, particularly when measured by any tests other than superficial.

The following points are specifically underlined by the seven-man executive board of the Alliance:

1. *That disappointing results have frequently followed when missionary boards or directors have failed to study the needs of the field "in consultation with well-known and experienced leaders before sending out their candidates."*

2. *That churches and missionary bodies abroad should give more thought to "the quality of the worker sent to the field."* For example, in a country with an ancient culture and a proud history it is a rare person indeed who can overcome the handicap of what is known in English-language circles as "butchering the Queen's English." (Its equivalent in this case might be called "crunching the Castilian.")

3. *That a narrow sectarianism works harmful results that are particularly noticeable in a land where the total Protestant community is a small minority.* "When the missionary has been welcomed as a fellow worker and then has behaved like a narrow-minded fanatic," the Spanish brethren find it deplorable.

4. *Pastoral and evangelistic work should, with rare exceptions, be left to the nationals.* This means that "candidates from abroad should be fitted to carry out tasks for which few nationals are prepared, and we think especially of Bible teaching and administration. This, however, demands outstanding gifts, preparation, and linguistic ability." It is pointed out that the supranational character of New Testament missionary effort, in which little or no account was taken of the nationality of the worker, but only of his calling and gifts, was made possible by the fact that the Roman Empire was largely a cultural unit, with Hellenistic Greek serving as a widely understood medium of expression. This differs markedly from the contemporary scene in which language barriers are not easy to surmount, either from the point of view of communications or of cultural implications.

5. *Identification with the people is a principle so manifestly essential to effective witness that failure here is all but fatal.* "Whatever the foreign missionary does, he must be prepared to fit into

the national, cultural, and social background of the people, strenuously avoiding the tendency to implant extraneous modes of thought and customs which are not biblical but merely 'foreign.' "

6. *Proselytism has peculiarly harmful and misleading effects in a country like Spain, where religious toleration is limited by law in such a way that, theoretically, "it applies only to people who are already Evangelicals."* "This means that missions generally begin new work in Spain at the expense of those who have borne the burden in past years, and some have been guilty of unscrupulously 'buying' existing work on the basis of 'who can offer most.' "

The statement concludes with a constructive plea for the recognition of three principles by those undertaking missionary work in Spain: (1) *consultation* (before a new effort is begun), (2) *co-ordination* (while it is in process), and (3) *consolidation* (as an effect and end). The significance of the third principle is pointed up by reference to "widely advertised campaigns" which, while they may do "some real service," may also be "divisive in tendency or transitory in their effects because they do not tend to the consolidation of the already established local churches and these should be the main channel for the development of future work."

This summary, which does less than justice to the statement as a whole, will indicate the acute importance of a more sensitive and objective approach to the work of missions worldwide, but especially in a difficult sector such as Spain.

Men of evangelical conviction and vast good will have spoken with conscience and care. They deserve to be heard.

Missions Today: Minuses and Pluses

Three things—the number is arbitrary, since more could be named—are presently hurting the cause of missions:

1. *The hangover of colonialism's mentality.*

It's the mission board "at home" that still insists on laying down the law for the Christian nationals overseas. It's the missionary on the field who still operates in the old maturity-immaturity pattern. He is paternalistic, condescending, and, in cases, unconsciously resentful of the emerging national leadership.

2. *The supersensitiveness of nationals who are reacting against foreign control.*

Understandably, they are in some degree influenced by the secular nationalism around them, with its often fierce anti-colonial, anti-white bias and bitterness. "Understandably" is used with deliberation. When the shoe was on the other foot, in the era when the colonialists were preening themselves, it was the missionaries who absorbed "the spirit of the times." In a book on *Colonialism and Christian Missions,* Bishop Stephen Neill writes:

> It was difficult for the missionary not to be affected by the unpleasantly blatant imperialism of the dying nineteenth century, not to assume that what was good for the West must necessarily be good for India also, not to accept without question the superiority of western to eastern man, and so to prejudice the effectiveness of his Christian witness by harmful irrelevances.

We are thus cautioned to go slow in our criticism of Christian nationals who appear overzealous to take the indigenous church right out of the hands of the Western missionary.

3. *The lack of resort to, and dependence upon, the Holy Spirit.*
There is an implicit humanism in today's bouncy, "schemy,"

programmatic Christianity that is curiously foreign both to the claim and to the climate of the New Testament. The first-century Church, embarking on a course of action, said unashamedly, "For it has seemed good to the Holy Spirit and to us" (Acts 15:28). Proposing that kind of confession would make a lot of twentieth-century churchmen as nervous as a cat on a hot tin roof. Our sophistication makes us content to say, "It has seemed good to us."

Twenty years ago Dr. E. Stanley Jones wrote, regarding Christendom generally, "We are presenting a Holy-Spiritless Christianity —a demand without a dynamic." And he added, "In an exposition [no author or title given] of preaching values in the Acts up to the sixty-fifth page the Holy Spirit was not mentioned. Pentecost had been skirted. It was all very brilliant, but it was moonlight instead of sunlight."

Make the Holy Spirit himself an irrelevancy, and you will make the Church's work a futility.

Enough of negation and fault-finding! Let me now name three things that I believe are currently at work to aid and forward the cause of missions:

1. *A growing appreciation of the Church and of its indispensable place and potency in world evangelization.*

Recently, in Peru, I listened to the Rev. Ruben Lores in an address on the principles that underlie Evangelism-in-Depth. His emphasis upon the Church—the total community of believers—was unmistakable. Furthermore, he rightly implied that the historic Christian communions—Lutherans, Anglicans, Methodists, Presbyterians, and others—must not be excluded from participation in evangelistic enterprise because they are presumed by certain evangelicals to be apostate. It needs to be recognized that the quest for a pure church, however desirable, is in the end futile. Such a church appears neither in the New Testament nor in subsequent church history. The principle of the remnant, moreover, must always be seen in the purpose of God wherever the varied structures of His Israel appear. He works through a redemptive minority to achieve His ends.

2. *An increasing impatience with Western-style denominational-ism.*

It is our view that the unbiblical character of denominational pluralism does not arise from the mere fact that variant groups exist. It is to be located in the implied claim of each denomination that it faithfully mirrors what God means by His Church. For the historic denominations to look over their fences and call the newer denominations "sects" is a rather fantastic piece of presumption. All of our denominations are sects: they are cuttings, or sections, of the Christian community.

Even the older denominations, despite their longer history and higher prestige, often appear to Asian and African Christians as highly sectarian bodies, whose historical peculiarities have far less to commend them than Europeans and North Americans presume to believe. Instead of Western wailing over this phenomenon, there should be thanks to God for it. It is a hopeful sign when the emerging groups of the mission world show impatience with the sectarianism of the West and seek for forms of Christian witness that speak of an authentic unity in Christ.

3. *A mounting feeling that a verbal Christian witness must be sanctioned and sustained by a convincing Christian presence.*

A generation ago one of our excellent missionary societies organized and carried through a colossal scheme for reaching every home in Japan with a portion of Scripture and a tract on the way of salvation. One of the unhappy by-products of this achievement, which had indeed many happy consequences, was the impression made upon many people in the United States and Canada that Japan had been evangelized. The fleeting Christian proclamation is not enough; there must be the abiding Christian presence: churches that are alive and multiplying, witnessing, worshiping, serving, persuading.

Missionary minuses and pluses! Let's not be disheartened by the former nor made overconfident by the latter.

Fanatics: A New Approach

It was, I believe, the Spanish philosopher George Santayana who once defined fanaticism as "the redoubling of your effort after you have forgotten your aim." By that test the contemporary world of missions is not beyond the danger of going fanatical.

Take a case in point. Not long ago the *International Review of Missions* reproduced an address given by Dr. Tracey K. Jones, Jr., associate general secretary of the World Division of the Board of Missions of The Methodist Church. "For 40 years," said Dr. Jones, "our Board has lived with the same Aim of Mission. Some have said that John R. Mott wrote it: 'The supreme aim of missions is to make the Lord Jesus Christ known to all peoples in all lands as their divine Savior, to persuade them to become his disciples, and to gather these disciples into Christian churches, to enlist them in the building of the Kingdom of God; to co-operate with these churches, to promote world Christian fellowship; and to bring to bear on all human life the spirit and principles of Christ!' "

Aside from what some would feel is the unbiblical reference to "building" the "Kingdom of God," the statement is clear and concise, orderly and comprehensive. Most importantly, it chimes with our Lord's own putting of the matter in the Matthew account of the Great Commission (28:18-20).

Let it be carefully noted that the foregoing statement of aim does not confine evangelization within the narrow limits of *words,* as though proclaiming the gospel could be adequately done by a verbal formula. Dr. Mott and our Methodist friends have been guided by a statement that has in-depth implications. It holds that the missionary *intention* is to "make the Lord Jesus Christ known to all peoples in all lands as their divine Savior." The means by which this is brought about—formal preaching, informal conversations, acts of neighborliness, ministries of healing, witness to social justice—may, and must, vary, but whatever these means may be the central intention remains authentically there: to "persuade" men to become Christ's "disciples," to gather them into the fellowship of His Church, and to relate them to the world of need in services that will "bring to bear on all human life the spirit and principles of Christ."

The statement, we believe, is worthy. No infallibility of phrasing is claimed for it. It is simply insightful and impelling.

But now, sharply in contrast, stands another analysis of the Christian mission in the world. Authored by a member of the German Missions Council, it too has recently appeared in the *International Review of Missions*.

Dr. Gunter Linnenbrink begins with the acknowledgment that historically "there is almost unanimous agreement that by 'mission' we are to understand the proclamation of the gospel and that by 'service' we are to understand the practice of Christian love-of-our-neighbor by Christian acts." "Seen in this light," he concedes, "the priority of mission seems to me to be indisputable."

At this point Dr. Linnenbrink throws down the gauntlet. "But this assumption itself," he declares, "is open to question." "The aim of missions," he continues, "must include the changing of social structures in order to insure greater justice, efforts for world peace and similar concrete acts—for, although they are only temporal and constantly threatened, these things are nevertheless expressions of the Kingdom of God." Continuing, he says: "God has not restricted nis work of salvation to the Church, still less to the human soul. He wants to be present in the whole world; He wants to save man as a unity of mind, soul and body. . . . But this means that concrete obedience—helping to build up God's kingdom by making a stand for law, freedom, justice and humanity —is not merely an appendage of faith; it is a sign of the ultimate establishment of His Kingdom as a concrete reality."

If Dr. Linnenbrink were seeking only to administer a rebuke to certain sectors of the Christian community for failure to bear a vigorous and sensitive social witness, his effort could be applauded. As matters stand, however, I can make little more than a muddle out of what he says.

Is there something here that is symptomatic of a spreading theological climate? Why this belittling of conversion, of discipling, of church-planting? Why this avoidance—studied or otherwise—of the New Testament tension between a world that is potentially redeemed in virtue of Christ's death and resurrection and at the same time a world that is actually alienated and doomed—requiring a repentance that cuts across pride and commitment to Christ that liberates life?

Here, I am afraid, we are in the throes of a theological confusion that cannot be separated from the quest for Christian unity.

The Santayana brand of fanaticism is threatening.

The Threat of the Cultic

When form becomes a fetish and a formula becomes a password, a cult is in the making, if indeed it has not already arrived.

How much of today's Christianity, whether in the traditional churches of the West or the generally newer communions of Africa and Asia, is becoming cultic?

An eminent Indian churchman, writing about Christianity on the Indian scene, declares:

> Both in the city and the village the Christian goes to his church on Sundays and is happy in the "Christian ghetto." He pays what he can for its support. He meets fellow Christians and is generally happy in their presence. But this sense of oneness often does not arise from their oneness in Christ. The Chris-

tian caste or communal basis is the stronger bond of union. After the Sunday service each returns to the unhappy world where he either forgets about his Sunday Christianity or leaves it aside for the sake of convenience. Normally he is not bothered about the fact that he has to live his religion all the days of the week. He is not usually any different in his office from his non-Christian friends. He too wastes much of his office time by idling or by gossiping. Of course there are exceptions. But exceptions also can be found among secularists and followers of other religions.

Note the devastating sequence: "goes to his church on Sundays . . . is not bothered by the fact that he has to live his religion all the days of the week." This is not evangelic; it is cultic.

Thirty-three factory and office workers, all of them professedly Christian, came together for an informal conference. A report of the meetings included the following:

> During the discussions most of the participants made it clear that they never felt any sense of responsibility or duty in their work. . . . One of the questions for group discussion was "How can we point others in our offices to our Master?" Many of the participants thought that this was an irrelevant question. "Tell us who the Master is. We do not know the Master," was the answer of many Christian employees. And most of these were regular communicant members of the church!

Let's not be deceived. When carrying the name "Christian" can have so little bearing on the stuff and shape of daily living, when it has ceased to generate distinctive motivations, when it no longer issues in behavior patterns that are creatively and convincingly different from those of society in general, then Christianity, in the measure in which this is true, has gone cultic. No longer a life-force, it has become a residual form. It is more of an escape from reality than an engagement with reality.

What is true at the broad level of Christian practice is similarly true in the narrower field of doctrinal orthodoxy. Necessary and useful is zeal for the theological "purity of the Church." "The faith once delivered to the saints" is not to be left to the small mercy of the innovators and the deviators. It must have defenders.

Here enters the peril. Saying the right words, repeating the proper phrases, clinging to the correct formulas, becomes the magical key to acceptance in orthodox circles. But the orthodoxy that *believes* soundly without the orthopraxy that *behaves* soundly is "sounding brass and a tinkling cymbal." It may be, in particular circumstances, a graver offense to the Almighty than creedal error.

A stout warrior for the "fundamentals," having prepared a public attack on a minister whose orthodoxy he challenges, has his attention called to certain inaccuracies in the charges he is getting ready to make. His defense for refusing to bring his proposed attack into line with the facts: he had prepared his manuscript and it was too late now to revise it!

When an ethically cloudy orthodoxy is content if only the right words are rightly pronounced, then the Christianity it represents has turned cultic.

How can this drift toward the cultic be reversed? Three things would immensely help:

1. *To dig into the New Testament with freshness, vigor, and confidence.* All over the world there is too much reading about Christianity and too little study of its one authoritative source book. On the mission fields this need includes that of producing simple commentaries for the use of the least educated but literate Christians. They must know firsthand the practical effects, as well as the faith-benefits, of the gospel.

2. *To get rid of the illusion that all church members are "in Christ."* To be in the Christian tradition is never a value to be despised. To be "in Christ" is more: it is a vitality—a gift of new life—for which there is no substitute. It is here that religious education makes a poor showing compared with conversion. Of the changed person, made new in Christ, it has been said: "It is not his wits that win but his life and witness."

3. *To face the grim possibility that Christianity, in wide areas of its influence, can fail in this century as it has failed in earlier centuries.* This is not the same as saying that Christ's Church can be destroyed. We have His own pledge that this will never be. But

it is to say that as North Africa was once a vast area of Christian work and witness and was succeeded by an alien faith, so the cultic, sentimental, irrelevant, unconvincing Christianity found in too many quarters today may be "cast out and trodden under foot of men." Tangless and tasteless, like salt without worth, it is rejected.

A picture one dreads to contemplate is that of a religious community clutching at its orthodoxy while it withers in its futility.

The Cross, the Cash, and the Commission

With a twinkle in his eye, Borden Parker Browne, the Boston University philosopher, once called philosophy chiefly "a disease of words." Words can be twisty and tricky, as in the case, years ago, of a small flour mill in the Upper Midwest that advertised on its stationery, "Next to the Largest Flour Mill in the World." The slogan rested, tongue in cheek, on the fact that this company's little mill stood on property that adjoined what at that time was the world's biggest mill.

More sophisticated but not more deceptive are today's communications techniques, which come (if you wish) complete with Madison Avenue's "hidden persuaders" and Marshall McLuhan's glossy (though often "guessy") explanations.

If anybody cares to be straightforward about it, it comes down to this: Words are supposed to have meanings, but if the same word means different things to different people, what can result other than confusion?

For specific illustration, take the word "stewardship." Some of our Bible translators, far from befriending us, only befog us. Open the Authorized Version to Luke 16:1, and you read, "There was a certain rich man, which had a *steward.*" But open your New English Bible to the same verse, and you will read, "There was a rich man who had a *bailiff.*" The trouble is that on the U. S. A. side of the ocean a "bailiff" is not a managing trust officer; he is a minor courtroom functionary.

Whatever our terminology, we need *to capture the stewardship insight.* Whether we use "steward" or "bailiff," the Greek word from which it comes means (1) an administration, and/or (2) an administrator. A steward is one who is given, who manages, and who must render an account for, a trust.

Is this the point where we begin to talk about money? Far from it! This is the point where we must get straight on something more ruthlessly basic than money. To the informed and committed Christian the whole of earth and of life is a trust from God, to be received gratefully and to be used responsibly. God is the owner; we are the owned. This is true of our world: "The earth is the Lord's" (Ps. 24:1). It is true of ourselves: ". . . Ye are not your own" (I Cor. 6:19). Just the twin fact that we are creatures and God is the Creator should be proof enough that all of us are tenants, not owners. We are managers, not originators.

The Apostle Paul, however, added to this concept of trusteeship the supreme Christian dimension when he wrote: "For ye are bought with a price; therefore glorify God in your body, and in your spirit, which are God's." For the Christian, therefore, the Cross of Christ means the revaluation of all values and the casting of the whole of life into the form of debt.

> Jesus paid it all,
> All to Him I *owe.*

Hence the United Stewardship Council of the United States and Canada was justified when, some years ago, it defined stewardship as "a consciously accepted philosophy of relationship between God and man which makes for activity for God *on the basis of obligation.*"

Here, then, is the insight we need: stewardship is not the leaving of a tip on God's tablecloth; it is the confession of an un-payable debt at God's Calvary.

The stewardship insight leads logically—and costingly—*to the stewardship imperative.* Paul put it this way to the Corinthian Christians: "Moreover, it is required in stewards that a man be found faithful." It is *required!*

The current crop of Protestants shuns "musts" as it shuns a plague. To our shame! We whine for our rights and whimper about our duties.

Slice it any way you will, Christians are men and women who are under bonds to Christ. When the sense of stewardship pos-sesses them, they know that they are not only to be responsible to God for every dollar *spent* but to be responding to God in every dollar *made.* The acquiring of wealth, no less than the giving of it, comes within the compass of stewardship.

Something, moreover, needs to be said about the *stewardship indicator.* In the Old Testament it was the tithe. In the New Testament it is the tithe *plus.* This plus makes it *grace* rather than *law,* and *token* rather than *sum.* Instead of saying that tithing makes a steward, it is far closer to the gospel truth to say that stewardship makes a tither.

Recently we saw a Christian businessman given a citation as "Layman of the Year." It was announced that nine-tenths of his income is set aside for Christian causes. One-tenth for living ex-penses and nine-tenths for Kingdom-of-God investment! This is what might be called "planned poverty." The wealth to which it leads has no index on Wall Street. It consists of redeemed lives, the world around, made possible by the holy materialism of consecrated cash.

Our Lord's commission to go and "make disciples" carries with it the obligation to make money (or its equivalent in goods) an agent of mission. We cannot serve God *and* mammon. What we can do is to serve God *with* mammon.

Is God Finished with White Missionaries?

Is God finished with white missionaries? The answer, of course, is No. God is not finished with anything that He is doing in His Church and in His world. Nor will He be finished until that climactic day of which Paul speaks when he says, "Then comes the end, when he [Christ] delivers the kingdom to God the Father after destroying every rule and every authority and power" (I Cor. 15:24).

But *means* and *ends,* however closely related, must not be confused. God is sovereign in the use of His means just as He is sovereign in the announcement of His ends. He putteth down one and setteth up another.

God has made large use of the white missionary. This is a fact that no future reading of history can possibly deny. But the signs are not lacking that we are entering a period when the missionary with the "pale face" will have no more than a limited role, and even that will be played under handicaps.

Reasons for this are numerous, and some of them are complex. To attempt an analysis of them is far from our present purpose.

Just one of these reasons calls for mention here. We shall allow it to emerge in a quotation drawn from the lips of an African. A Nigerian university student said to a European missionary, "If you didn't have a tendency to give a patronizing pat on the back, we would feel less resentful towards you."

The catch is in that word "patronizing."

Modern history did something with the white man that made him a conqueror in a dozen realms. But the psychological legacy left to him by this conquest has now come home to plague him. It takes the form of a complacency with himself and a condescendingness towards the colored races of which, half the time, he is not even aware. And, of course, therein lies the pathos of it.

There is, to be sure, a cure for this subtly masked prejudice and pride. But it is costly. It means a radical disentanglement from the cultural web in which we Caucasians are caught. It means our taking seriously the revolutionary position to which Paul had come: "From now on, therefore, we regard no one from a human point of view; even though we once regarded Christ from a human point of view, we regard him thus no longer. Therefore, if anyone is in Christ, he is a new creation; the old has passed away, behold, the new has come. All this is from God, who through Christ reconciled us to himself and gave us the ministry of reconciliation" (II Cor. 5:16-18.)

Where then is boasting? Where is patronizing? Where is condescension?

Instead—"I am debtor," or, as J. B. Phillips has it, "I owe something to all men, from cultured Greek to ignorant savage" (Rom. 1:14).

Arab and Jew: A Missionary Reflection

Consider this scene:

It was 1967. The Israeli-Arab war was in all the headlines. A colleague of mine was having lunch with two Christian friends. To them he put the question: Suppose a Jew and an Arab were to enter the room. Would you as a Christian feel that God has more love for one than for the other? One replied No. The other said that God would have greater love for the Israeli.

How *Christian* is that answer?

Or this:

The day after the cease-fire went into effect I was riding with a Christian brother in his car. He was thrilled by Israel's victory over the Arabs. He said that the swift and overwhelming way in which Israel crushed the Arabs reminded him of the manner in which God gave victory to the children of Israel in Joshua's and in David's day. It was implied that since God was *for* the Israelis and *against* the Arabs, the victory of the Israelis was a foregone conclusion.

Responsible interpretation

How biblical is this thinking? Is it emotionally conditioned or is it well grounded theologically? Also, does it rest, so far as the relevant scriptures are concerned, in a clear and undisputed exegesis of those scriptures?

To go back to the first World War, was the Balfour Declaration of the British government, which came out openly in favor of a national home for the Jewish people, politically defensible *because* Israel's return to Palestine was predicted in Holy Scripture? If so, one of the scriptures to be cited would be Genesis 15:18, which tells us that "the Lord made a covenant with Abraham, saying, Unto thy seed have I given this land."

But immediately there are problems. If we take this literally and unconditionally, then the Arabs, who also are of the "seed" of Abraham, can lay claim to the "land." Yet such a conclusion, we are reminded, is forbidden by Genesis 21:12, "In *Isaac* shall thy seed be called." Correct. But the moment that this is seen and acknowledged, we have made a concession. We have conceded that the original promise was not *exactly* literal, but only *qualifiedly* so. For if the line of inheritance, with respect to the land, is now to be restricted to Isaac, then not only Ishmael but five other sons of Abraham who were born after Isaac are to be stricken from the "seed" roll.

Nor is this all. Isaac's brother Esau was as much the seed of Abraham as Isaac himself. Yet he is excluded from the promise of a share in the land. But this exclusion, we are told, is to be understood in the light of Genesis 25:34, where we are informed that "Esau despised his birthright," selling it away for a "mess of pottage." Difficulties, however, are not so easily resolved. For if this be the case, then the promise made to Abraham is not, as we have seen, exactly literal, nor is it absolutely unconditional.

Perplexing distinction

As for Paul's word in Romans 9:13, "Jacob I loved, but Esau I hated," it appears in a context in which God's sovereignty over history is being treated, and that always calls upon us to remove our shoes since we are in the presence of holy mysteries. Let two things be affirmed with confidence: (1) that the verbs "loved" and "hated," far from having the emotional overtones appropriate to fallen man, have the force of "accepted" and "rejected"; and (2) that what is primarily in view is not *God's merciful offer of saving grace* but *God's sovereign right to select for service.*

By His own choice and for His own glory, God chose to work through the line of Isaac in raising up a people whose singular service would be to say to the whole world of idolatry, "The Lord our God is one Lord, and him only shalt thou worship."

The same parallel does not prevail, however, with respect to the second form of service for which Esau was rejected and Isaac selected. "The Deliverer will come from Zion," Paul declares in Romans 11:26. It was from the Isaac-Israel line of Abraham's seed that the Hebrew Messiah and the world's Redeemer was to come.

Through her leaders Israel rejected Christ as the Messiah. The result has been both melancholy and merciful: melancholy because of the long-continued refusal of most members of the Jewish community to confess Christ as Son of God, Lord of glory, and Savior of men; merciful because, within the new covenant of grace and within the ample fold of the Christian church, there is a place for all the sons and daughters of Israel who will confess the saving action of God in the Cross and Resurrection of Jesus Christ.

Undiscriminating obligation

The evangelistic and missionary dimension of this truth should be apparent, though it is not always so in fact. The new covenant of grace is open to all—Jew, Arab, Gentile. The love of God that blazes like a towering beacon from the Cross of Calvary is offered to all. It is as accessible to Arabs as to Jews.

And if Jews corporately have a large place in God's future purpose, let not Christians think that they or their political leaders are appointed to help the Almighty carry out his purposes. Our task is to provide for Jews and Arabs alike a living demonstration of that respect we should give them as fellow creatures of God and that love we owe them under the compulsion of Calvary.

At the Cross the ground is level. "There is no difference!"

PART V

MISSION IS PEOPLE

Let's Speak Up for Training

"The first missionary book I ever bought cost a penny. It was called *The Preparation of Missionaries*. I didn't read it. An old missionary assured me that it would be beyond me."

So speaks Dr. H. C. Lefever, of the London Missionary Society, bringing forward a reminiscence from more than fifty years ago. He eventually got to the mission field and there learned the hard way what are the "do's" and "don'ts" of effective service.

There are still those—fortunately a diminishing number—who say to the pastor or the missionary executive: "Tell me, why does Bill Brown have to take any more training? He has his M.D. He feels called to medical missions. We all know him to be a fine Christian. If the need out there is so great, why can't he leave now, and get on with the job that needs doing?"

Or the person in question may be a nurse, a teacher, a linguist, an evangelist. Regardless of the form that the missionary vocation is to take, what is there about it that makes special preparation important?

Let's not beat about the bush: without such training the missionary recruit simply doesn't know enough. This is true in at least three directions:

1. *He doesn't know enough about the world to which he is going.* It is the world of the Asian, or the African, or the Latin. Modes of behavior that seem silly to a North American are not silly in the context of those customs that prevail in the culture to which one is going.

Of more importance, and less easily acquired, is knowledge of the contemporary social, political, and economic factors that are shaping the lives of the people to whom the missionary is going. In a Latin American country a missionary wife told me, with grave dismay, that the national university was "a hotbed of communism." From better informed sources I learned that there was indeed a cell of hard-core Communists on the campus but that most of the agitation represented a knowledgeable protest against the corruptions and exploitations of the wealthy power structure in a country devoid of a healthy middle class. Missionaries who ignorantly or deliberately isolate themselves from perceptive concern about these seething social situations will have little influence in Latin America's world of tomorrow. I am far from suggesting that they must attempt direct political involvement, but rather that they must undersand the climate in which revolutionary changes are taking place.

Peter Wagner, amid the tensions and trauma of Bolivian life, says rightly, in the *Evangelical Missions Quarterly:* "All these things mean that if we are to keep up with the social revolution, we will need to permit a revolution in our own thinking."

2. *The missionary recruit needs training because he doesn't know enough about the history of missions.* Even a nurse or a doctor who accepts the missionary vocation needs the immense enlightenment that comes from studying such a volume as Stephen Neill's *History of Missions.* By universal acknowledgment, missionaries have done utterly splendid things; by their own admission, missionaries have done utterly stupid things. We of today

should know something about *both* as they speak their lessons out of the past.

Historically, how has it come about that for much more than a hundred years we have had (a) the churches in mission, (b) the church-related missionary society in mission, and (c) the independent missionary society in mission?

Whether this is good or bad, theologically defensible or otherwise, we should know how it has developed. With this knowledge as a backdrop, we should be prepared to understand why, in mission areas where an indigenous church is maturing, the whole question of the relationship between the "churches" and the "missions" is now wide open, and the pressure is on for solutions that nobody finds it easy to achieve.

3. *Furthermore, the new missionary needs special preparation because he doesn't know himself well enough.* The self he knows (at least in part) is one that has probably developed in a protected environment: a home where he is loved, a church where he "belongs," a community in which he is accepted, a racial milieu (assuming that he is white) in which he is part of the "in" group.

But how much does he know of the self that must now function in a new cultural and religious situation? Here, for example, his relationship to the national church may be ill-defined and its congeniality cannot be taken for granted. Here, for a while at least, he may have to live with the feeling that he is needed but not wanted.

Four hundred missionary dropouts in twenty-five years is the record of one of our historic denominations, according to a self-study made by this group. Under "health" and "psychological" causes come such items as (a) crises early in the missionary's experience, (b) friction among missionaries, (c) frustration over meager results, (d) disagreement with mission policy, (e) misunderstandings with national Christians, and others.

It is easy for some of us to believe that many missionaries could have been saved from a lost career by a course of in-residence training, such as may be had at Missionary Internship near Detroit and Missionary Orientation Center at Stony Point, New York. For the greater glory of the God whose mission we serve, let's not balk at thoroughness of preparation.

Christian Infiltrators

Not long ago the government of Egypt was advertising for technical and professional assistants in certain of its departments. It was willing to take them from abroad. A missionary of the Church Missionary Society wrote to London, inquiring:

> Could not some committed Christians from elsewhere come to Egypt to these educational (or industrial) posts which are available to people with the right qualifications? Could we not put this challenge to some of the Christians in Britain? They would find an opportunity of a meeting place with the ordinary person as well as university students.

The general secretary of the CMS, the Rev. John Taylor, commented:

> We certainly believe that our Society is called today to offer the largely invisible and inward links of its supportive fellowship to just such people as that writer has in mind, and that, in our parlance, "CMS missionaries" should embrace on equal terms those who seek appointment under governments or universities overseas as well as those who serve in some Church appointment, provided only their desire to uplift Jesus Christ before men is paramount.

Add to this the fact that in 1966 President Nasser had told the Egyptian people that their national security and well-being demanded "unselfish human beings," people of "efficiency, capacity, and character."

No one needs to remind me that Mr. Nasser, in the eyes of some people, could do with more of these qualities himself. Nevertheless, Nasser, like Indira Gandhi of India and President Marcos of the Philippines, is threatened by a cancerously spreading inefficiency and corruption in government. He at least discerns what sort of persons are required to save the day.

Here then—in Africa, Asia, and Latin America—are places where the unconventional missionary has an opening. Not a big opening, nor a frequent one, but an opening just the same.

Have we Christian infiltrators who are prepared to move in?

When it comes to the forms of Christian witness, new ground must be broken, new entries made, new chances taken.

Too long have Christians in African and Asian countries given the impression that they are an island of piety, scarcely washed by the seas of the nation's surrounding life and action. Foreignness can never be completely disclaimed by the expatriates from Europe and North America, but something can be done to lift this stigma from the Christian community in mission lands. Perhaps infiltration in the spheres of business and government is one way of doing it.

It's worth considering!

Navigator and Collaborator

I have known him for several years. More than once, while I was flying from one place to another in India, he has been up there in the cockpit of the plane on which I was traveling.

He is a navigator in the employ of Indian Airlines.

But that is not all that he is. He is an infectiously enthusiastic Indian Christian, whose witness for Christ is carried into every activity and area of his life.

Nor is that all. He is the lay leader of the large Methodist Church in Madras,[1] where it has been my privilege to be engaged in a preaching mission.

But that is not all. He is an avid reader of the best books, especially if they contribute to a better understanding of the Bible.

Nor is that the full story. His employment schedule is such that occasionally he has as much as three or four days of free time. During these times he has been teaming up with his pastor, Dr. Samuel Kamaleson, in short evangelistic missions in other cities. While the pastor does the preaching at night, this layman gives Bible studies for other laymen in the early mornings.

This splendid coaction on the part of pastor and layman, in one four-day mission, resulted in more than three hundred confessions of faith!

Salute John Richard: airline navigator and evangelistic collaborator!

Clergy, Crisis, and Candor

Item: A Christian father in rural India writes to a city pastor, pleading, "My son, brought up in our very poor home, is coming to your city to try to enter teachers' college. If he fails, please help him to get into theological college." Says the pastor in re-

---

[1] John Richard, no longer a navigator, is now the pastor's full-time assistant.

ply: "Unfortunately I cannot subscribe to the view that poverty and inferiority are qualifications eminently desirable in one who is to be an ambassador for the King of kings."

Item: "We must honestly face the fact that Africa, even Christian Africa, no longer looks to the Christian ministry for spiritual leadership. Why has this happened? It has happened because the Church has not cared enough for her own ministry." (*The Crisis in the Christian Ministry in Africa,* published by the All Africa Conference of Churches.)

Item: ". . . There is a gradual deterioration in the 'brand-image' of the pastor. In a number of recent conferences with clergy (in Africa and Asia) I have been struck by the general disappointment they show in their own sons, few of whom even contemplate ordination or full-time service of any description with the Church. This is hardly surprising if they have grown up watching a father trying to claim a status which few are prepared to accord him any longer." (Douglas Webster, professor of missions in Selly Oak Theological College in England, in the *International Review of Missions.*)

Let's face it: In most of the Christian world, whether in the western hemisphere or the eastern, the ordained ministers are in a state of declining status and of reduced effectiveness. To be sure, there are compensating facts and factors. One of them is the growing conviction that, as the Anglicans put it ten years ago at the Lambeth Conference, there is "too sharp a distinction between clergy and laity." Protestants are beginning to realize that clergy-lay relationships must be rescued from the caste system that has grown up around them. In Douglas Webster's words, "Just as the whole Church *is* the laity, so the whole laity *has* a ministry and *is* a priesthood." True and timely!

We nevertheless face the irreducible fact that "pastors" and "teachers" are offices in the New Testament Church. Their function and responsibility are far more important considerations than any finicky discussion about a "proper" or "valid" way of ordaining those who fill these offices. Their primary task is "to equip God's people for work in his service" (Eph. 4:12, NEB). The *effective* ministry of the whole Church requires the *equipping* ministry of that part of the Church which is clergy.

And here is the rub. By and large, the pastors are simply not engaged in the serious business of equipping the people they serve to communicate the claims and offers of Jesus Christ. The clergy is to serve the Church in order that the Church may serve the world. When this sequence miscarries, as it too frequently does, it will be found that the pastoral ministry is too possessive and the congregational ministry too parochial. Both lack the disciplined outgoings by which they should be marked and motivated.

In Africa the absence of an adequate and alert ministerial leadership is particularly disturbing. Thus one who speaks for African Anglicanism can write: "Not only are there no more than a handful of graduate clergy, but the great majority have not had even a secondary school education. . . . It is in Africa that one minister so often has in his charge anything up to 50 or more congregations." In January, 1968, I was told by the head of the Africa Evangelical Church (a communion of some 1600 indigenous congregations) that their pastors are responsible for anything up to ten congregations apiece.

Undertrained and overworked—these are twin defects found in wide areas of African church life. The lack of adequate education is especially notable—and crippling—in the rapidly growing cities. A pastor who is effective in the village life of the bush country can rarely be expected to make the grade in any of the scores of Africa's burgeoning urban areas. In the University of Paris alone are more than six thousand African students who will soon be part of life in Lagos, Kinshasa, Nairobi, and Lusaka. They will not be challenged by bush preaching or by the moralistic scoldings of taboo-minded pietists. A competent use of the vernacular and a responsible expounding of Holy Scripture, combined with the persuasive force of a radiant Christlikeness, must be found if these cultured nationals are to be won to Christ and His Way.

With respect to overwork, the crucial consideration is *definition* rather than *volume*. What do young people see in today's typical pastor? This is the question of a group of concerned African churchmen. "They see him too often as an itinerant dispenser of sacraments, a chairman of interminable committee meetings concerned with finance and buildings, a collector of subscriptions and tithes!" Granted, this image of the "organization man," the administrator who gives orders and disburses funds, has been passed on to the African by the missionary. Understanding the effect of historical circumstances is no substitute for putting right a mischievous condition. It will be disastrous if African pastors (and pastors everywhere) lose their way. Their primary role is not that of working *for* the laity but *with* them in order to inspire and instruct them.

It is probably fair to say that overcoming clergy scarcity is not as urgent as redefining clergy responsibility—abroad and at home.

Not Prima Donnas but Partners

Why is it that more young people in the United States—especially among the college-trained—are not offering themselves for missionary service overseas?

Charles H. Troutman, drawing on his years of service in Inter-Varsity Christian Fellowship, believes that one ingredient in the answer is a distorted image of the missionary's role that is too often given in the speeches of missionary executives and the reports of missionaries on furlough. The distortion arises through an overworking of the idea of *leadership*, conceived of in highly individualistic, if not heroic, terms.

Actually, says Troutman, "The typical student is less interested in becoming a heroic leader than he is in sacrificial service *as a member of a team*" (italics ours).

Today's college student has almost certainly become acquainted with students from overseas. One of them may be his roommate. Some of these visiting students are openly hostile to the Christian missions at work in their countries; others, especially if they are themselves Christians, are not bitterly negative but they are probably critical at points, sometimes shrewdly so, sometimes superficially so.

In any case, the Christian varsity student from one of our American churches has already come to realize (1) that there is a body of Christian nationals in existence in most of these overseas lands and (2) that the wave of the future does not favor U. S. citizens who go out to foreign fields to start something new, to assume leadership roles, to exercise authority over the nationals.

Many of these knowledgeable and sensitive college young people are more likely to be repelled than challenged by a missionary conference address that ignores the existence of the national churches and the importance of a fraternally and creatively meaningful relationship between the missionaries and the indigenous communities of Christians. It is in this context that we see the significance of the team idea which, Mr. Troutman insists, makes a far greater appeal to our college youth than one that is highly individualistic.

The truth is that unless the leader concept is blended and balanced with the servant concept, what we get can be more demonic than Christian. "To tell a man," says Bishop Stephen Neill, "that he is called to be a leader, or that he is being trained to be a leader, is the best way of insuring his spiritual ruin, since in the Christian world ambition is more deadly than any other sin, and, if it is yielded to, makes a man unprofitable in the ministry."

The cut and thrust of those words are sharp indeed, but no sharper than when Jesus said, "You know that in the world, rulers lord it over their subjects, and their great men make them feel the weight of authority; but it shall not be so with you. Among you, whoever wants to be great must be your servant, and whoever would be first must be the willing slave of all" (Matt. 20:25-27, New English Bible).

If Troutman is right, our Christian varsity friends will be more responsive if that note is more clearly and compellingly sounded.

Improved Means and Unimproved Ends

Consider the way in which, too often, we improve the means by which we do things without improving the quality of what we do with these means. The latest in television gadgetry and color moves us no farther along the road of progress unless what we send out is better in content than what we once communicated on a five-party line.

Looking into that future for communications, so startlingly portrayed by the board chairman of RCA (see page 78) Richard Tobin somberly asks: "How many dismal Westerns per night will flow by esoteric laser beam from Radio City to one of the emerging nations thirsting for American culture?" Improved means to unimproved ends!

Two thoughts arise at this point.

The central message of the gospel with which the Church is entrusted is the unimprovable *end* for which the best *means* of communication are not too good. Yet seldom do we find gospel radio, or television, or films, or publications, that are outstanding for technical excellence. There never was much excuse for this sloppiness; there is less than ever today.

But, secondly, why do we wait for the occasional day or hour when the gospel can be offered directly? Why do we not take seriously the responsibility of putting the Christian stamp on forms of expression, that are not traditional but which for our day may be, in the long run, as potent as a "Lutheran Hour" message or a "Back to the Bible" meditation?

Mr. J. Arthur Rank, Britain's famous movie magnate, told a friend that at one time he had dreamed of producing one really great religious film each year. "And why haven't you done it?" asked the friend. "Because," he replied, "to produce a notable religious film there must be Christian story writers, Christian producers, Christian actors and actresses, Christian cameramen." Sadly he added, "I cannot find enough of them."

Let young Christians, career-minded, take a long look at that statement. Let them apply it to art, music, journalism, books, radio, television. These are the constantly improved means. What remains is to bring them more nearly into harmony with the best ends.

The Links of Life

We were walking away from a Salvation Army center in São Paulo, Brazil. The iron gate through which we were to pass into the street suddenly admitted a young lady in Salvationist uniform. The major who was at our side introduced us. Where was she from? Yorkshire, in England. Had I seen Billy Graham recently? If I were going to see him soon, would I please convey her greeting. When we walked on, the major said, " I must tell you about this young lady." The gist of what he told me was this:

She was converted at Harringay, almost at the finish of the

London Crusade in 1954. She had grown up in the aura of aristocracy. Her father is addressed as "Sir," and her mother as "Lady." Not long after her conversion the voice of God said, "To the mission field!" Her parents were horrified. Nothing daunted her. After training, she came to Brazil. She has been stationed in one of the "toughest" (the word is the major's) towns in the nation. There, amid forbidding circumstances, Christ has worked through her, winning people to Himself. The police chief said, "You need special protection because you live alone. I will have a policeman assigned to watch your premises." She said, "It isn't necessary." He insisted. The policeman was sent. She led him to Christ. Since then the man's wife and two children have experienced conversion.

London and Brazil! On the map, far apart! In God's heart, close together!

London, where they said—and still say—that Dr. Graham's mass evangelism yields no permanent results! Brazil, where the firm and fruitful results show how little open to the facts some sophisticated minds can be!

"Christ-Intoxicated Missionaries"

It was this editor's privilege in June, 1965, to participate in the World Missions Conference which was held in Bournemouth, England, to commemorate the founding, in 1865, of the China Inland Mission. This society is now known as the Overseas Missionary Fellowship. Its origin and history are indissolubly linked with the name of Hudson Taylor.

At the age of thirty-three Taylor had seen enough of China to know that beyond the teeming coastal cities were vast provinces

—at least eleven of them without any missionary occupation—whose millions of people needed to hear the name of Christ.

Weary and half ill, the young missionary was on holiday at the seaside. "If God gives us a band of men for inland China," he wrote in his journal, "and they go, and all die of starvation, they will only be taken straight to heaven; and if only one heathen soul is saved, would it not be well worth while?"

Then came the decision to venture with God. Taylor wrote on a leaf in his Bible: "Prayed for twenty-four willing, skillful workers at Brighton, June 25, 1865." He added: "If we are obeying the Lord, the responsibility rests with Him, not with us!"

The first monetary gift to support the new enterprise amounted to $50. It was unsolicited. In the following ten decades $36 million, likewise unsolicited, have come pouring into the society's treasury. More than three thousand missionaries have been sent out.

Nothing that characterized the centenary conference at Bournemouth impressed me more than the unwillingness of the society's present leaders to consume huge amounts of time in extolling the past (or even bewailing it at points) and the determination, under God, to confront the present and future with resolute confidence and hope.

The spirit was reflected when the Fellowship took action to provide that in the future its ranks are to be opened to men and women of all races and nationalities. That is to say, an Indonesian Christian, feeling the call of God to missionary service in, let us say, Thailand, would be eligible for commissioning by the society, assuming of course that he met the qualifications normally asked of candidates.

The present general director of the Overseas Missionary Fellowship (who retires this year), the Rev. J. Oswald Sanders, is a man possessed by a resilient and forward-looking spirit. Realistically he declares: "All planning for the future must take cognizance of the patent fact that East Asia represents a turbulent scene of revolutionary change." Approvingly he quotes a leading Asian Christian who said to him:

We want many categories of missionaries, but remember, what we want is Christ-intoxicated missionaries. Please help us to get such people.

And that goes, in terms of need, for the whole world of missions!

PART VI

MISSION IS POWER

"The Boy Who Believes in the Holy Ghost"

Pentecost Sunday!

In Great Britain they call it Whitsunday.

Who cares?

If that sounds irreverent, it is no more so than the irreverence of neglect from which the day suffers in our American churches generally.

Britain's Dr. Norman Maclean used to recall an unintentionally amusing incident that occurred one day in the course of an examination at the Colinton Parish School. The teacher had required the class to memorize the Apostles' Creed, and to repeat it clause by clause, with each pupil having his own clause. As the recitation began, the first boy said, "I believe in God the Father Almighty, Maker of heaven and earth." The second boy said: "I believe in Jesus Christ his only Son our Lord." The recitation went on until it reached the point where one of the boys had said: "From thence he shall come to judge the quick and the dead." Then there fell a silence that indicated something had gone wrong. The silence was broken by the next boy in line, who said to the examiner: "Please, sir, the boy who believes in the Holy Ghost is absent today."

On which Dr. Maclean comments: "Lots of folks are absent when it comes to that clause."

So they are, alas!

Arthur Hurd says the doctrine of the Holy Spirit has been the "undiscovered country of Christianity, the dark continent of the Christian life, the land where our spiritual resources lie, but lie undeveloped."

Today some of our churches are beginning to rediscover those primal resources which are theirs in the person and power of the Spirit of God—but far from enough!

One thing we could now do is to examine, at greater depth, what the Bible says about the Holy Spirit.

Professor D. W. Dillistone, in the midst of a careful survey of the biblical data, makes the suggestion that in these two words— adjective and noun—we have a profound double symbol: "Holy . . . the symbol of an intense purity" and "Spirit . . . the symbol of a boundless grace."

In the Old Testament this connection may be traced in such a sequence as we have in Isaiah 6 and 61. In Chapter 6 the vivid and controlling focus is upon the holiness of the Lord: "Holy, holy, holy, is the Lord God of hosts." Here is the firm texture of what He essentially and eternally is.

But the focus of attention is different in Isaiah 61: "The Spirit of the Lord God is upon me; because the Lord hath anointed me to preach good tidings unto the meek; he hath sent me to bind up the broken-hearted, to proclaim liberty to the captives, and the opening of the prison to them that are bound" (v. 1).

Thus in the Holy Spirit we see one who is *firmly holy,* searching, judging, convicting; we see one who, at the same time, is *freely gracious,* heralding hope, healing the broken, liberating the enslaved.

As "holy," He leads a man to cry, "Woe is me"; as "Spirit," He leads a man to exclaim, "Here am I, send me."

Take another approach. In the life and work of our Lord this two-sidedness of the Holy Spirit is repeatedly in evidence. At work in Jesus, the *Holy* Spirit drives the money-changers from the temple and blazes out in hot condemnation of the scribes and Pharisees. But there is another side. At work in Jesus, the Holy *Spirit* welcomes home a penitent prodigal, binds up the wounds of a waylaid and battered traveler, and tenderly sends forth a woman of ill repute into the society of the forgiven.

Take note of this. it was not until the distinctive character of the Holy Spirit had been decisively revealed in the words and acts of Jesus Christ, not until the norm of the Spirit-filled life had been spelled out as a life that bears the likeness of Jesus, that it was possible for the Christian mission *in* and *to* the world to get under way. The risen Lord, on the day of His triumph, gave to this mission its simple, superb, summoning expression: "Receive the Holy Spirit. . . . As the Father has sent me, even so I send you" (John 20:22,21, RSV).

To sum it up, let the Holy Spirit of God freely work, in church or person, and three things will emerge: *sanctity, responsibility,* and *vivacity*.

Because He is the Spirit of holiness, He convicts of sin—sin in its refinements as well as its crudities, sin in its social subtleties as well as its personal sordidness.

Because He is the Spirit of grace, He heals and sends out the healed to be healers; He cleanses and sends out the cleansed to make holiness attractive, not repulsive. He breaks that He may make whole, and sends forth the broken-made-whole that they may wake up the proudly whole to their need of being broken.

And all of this—if Pentecost be present—takes place in a climate of incredible vivacity. The Spirit is wind and fire. His ministry is passionate. It need not be noisy but it cannot be prosy. It need not be traumatic, but it cannot be tepid. For, as the author of *Ecce Homo* put it long ago, "No heart is pure that is not passionate; no virtue is safe that is not enthusiastic."

Let's bring back "the boy who believes in the Holy Ghost"!

Don't Sleep Through The Revolution

Paul S. Rees

Is it possible to sleep through a revolution?

Unfortunately, yes.

Rip Van Winkle did it—he slept through the Revolutionary War. And John Doe Christian is doing it today—sound asleep in his comfortable pew while revolution rages on all fronts around him, in the church and in the world. He has forgotten that his Christianity is a revolutionary— and revolutionizing—one. Or else he prefers his revolution in safe and predictable forms!

In *Don't Sleep Through the Revolution*, Dr. Rees has sharpened his sword, not to cut anyone down, but to prick them awake